# Analyzing Analytics



*Analyzing Analytics: Disrupting Journalism One Click at a Time* critically examines how journalists use web analytics in their work and the implications of that use.

Now that web analytics has become deeply embedded in newsrooms, its impact on journalism is even more potent. Documenting the different ways in which web analytics has disrupted traditional journalism, the book provides a timely review of what we know so far about the place of web analytics in reporting, and maps a future research agenda. It conceptualizes web analytics as an object of journalism where audiences, businesses, technologists, and journalists confront one another, negotiating the contours of digital journalism in the process.

Including newly developed theoretical frameworks as well as case studies and empirical projects, the book is ideal for journalism students, researchers, and professional journalists.

**Edson C. Tandoc Jr.** is Associate Professor in the Wee Kim Wee School of Communication and Information, Nanyang Technological University, Singapore.

## Disruptions: Studies in Digital Journalism

*Series editor: Bob Franklin*

**Disruptions** refers to the radical changes provoked by the affordances of digital technologies that occur at a pace and on a scale that disrupts settled understandings and traditional ways of creating value, interacting and communicating both socially and professionally. The consequences for digital journalism involve far reaching changes to business models, professional practices, roles, ethics, products and even challenges to the accepted definitions and understandings of journalism. For Digital Journalism Studies, the field of academic inquiry which explores and examines digital journalism, disruption results in paradigmatic and tectonic shifts in scholarly concerns. It prompts reconsideration of research methods, theoretical analyses and responses (oppositional and consensual) to such changes, which have been described as being akin to 'a moment of mind blowing uncertainty'.

Routledge's new book series, ***Disruptions: Studies in Digital Journalism***, seeks to capture, examine and analyse these moments of exciting and explosive professional and scholarly innovation which characterize developments in the day-to-day practice of journalism in an age of digital media, and which are articulated in the newly emerging academic discipline of Digital Journalism Studies.

**Journalism Between the State and the Market**
*Helle Sjøvaag*

**Opting Out of Digital Media**
*Bonnie Brennen*

**Photojournalism Disrupted**
*Helen Caple*

For more information, please visit: https://www.routledge.com/Disruptions/book-series/DISRUPTDIGJOUR

"An incredibly accessible, critical, global, and in-depth assessment of how web analytics are changing journalism, written by one of the foremost scholars in the field."

—Folker Hanusch, PhD, University of Vienna, Austria

# Analyzing Analytics

## Disrupting Journalism One Click at a Time

**Edson C. Tandoc Jr.**

Routledge
Taylor & Francis Group
LONDON AND NEW YORK

First published 2019 by Routledge

2 Park Square, Milton Park, Abingdon, Oxon OX14 4RN
605 Third Avenue, New York, NY 10017

*Routledge is an imprint of the Taylor & Francis Group, an informa business*

First issued in paperback 2022



Publisher's Note

The publisher has gone to great lengths to ensure the quality of this reprint but points out that some imperfections in the original copies may be apparent.

*British Library Cataloguing-in-Publication Data*
A catalogue record for this book is available from the British Library

*Library of Congress Cataloging-in-Publication Data*
A catalog record has been requested for this book

ISBN: 978-1-138-49652-1 (hbk)
ISBN: 978-1-03-233835-4 (pbk)
DOI: 10.4324/9781138496538

Typeset in Times New Roman
by codeMantra

**To my parents, Edson Sr. and Perlita, and my siblings, Edson III, Edson IV, and Eloisa: Look, I wrote a book!**

# Contents

| | | |
|---|---|---|
| | *Preface: acknowledgments and reflections* | x |
| 1 | Disrupting journalism | 1 |
| 2 | Changing audiences | 11 |
| 3 | Overlapping fields | 23 |
| 4 | Journalists adapting | 36 |
| 5 | Changing journalism | 52 |
| 6 | Journalism disrupted | 69 |
| | *Index* | 79 |

# Preface

## Acknowledgments and reflections

Throughout this book, I will make the argument that web analytics is a platform where the interests of journalists, audiences, advertisers, and technologists intersect. The extent to which web analytics disrupts journalism is the product of how journalists negotiate these complementary and competing interests. The book also presents the intersection between my own research on web analytics, my collaborations with my colleagues and students, and my learnings from a lot of great work in this area. This book is the product of my experience as a journalist and my training as a journalism researcher as well as my interactions with practitioners and scholars who have been doing amazing work in understanding the use and impact of web analytics in the context of journalism.

This book draws heavily from my doctoral dissertation, which I completed at the University of Missouri in December 2013 (Tandoc, 2013). I was first introduced to the world of web analytics when I worked as research assistant for Mike Jenner. I helped him in conducting a survey among American newsroom managers to understand how their newsrooms were using web analytics (Jenner & Tandoc, 2013). It was also at the university where my doctoral supervisor, Tim P. Vos, introduced me to field theory as a framework for studying journalism. I worked as a newspaper reporter for six years prior to my doctoral studies, but I had never used web analytics. The more I learned about it, the more curious I became about how it could affect journalism. So, I decided to focus on web analytics for my dissertation. I visited three online newsrooms affiliated with legacy newspapers in the Midwest to observe and interview news workers about web analytics (Tandoc, 2014). I also subsequently conducted an online survey involving 206 online news editors in the United States (Tandoc, 2015).

I continued this line of research when I moved to Nanyang Technological University (NTU) in Singapore in January 2014. I also became involved in collaborative projects that investigated the use of web analytics in newsrooms across different countries. So, over the years, my understanding of web analytics' place in journalism was largely shaped by these research partnerships. Here are some of the people to blame: I collaborated with Ryan Thomas from the University of Missouri to reflect on the ethical dilemmas that web analytics presents (Tandoc & Thomas, 2014). I also conducted further surveys. One involved 360 online journalists in the United States and was for a project with Pat Ferrucci from the University of Colorado that sought to understand factors that lead journalists to using web analytics (Tandoc & Ferrucci, 2017). Another survey involved 356 news journalists in Australia, part of my collaboration with Folker Hanusch from the University of Vienna to examine the impact of web analytics use on journalistic role orientations (Hanusch & Tandoc, 2017).

I also took part in several qualitative research projects. I worked with Raul Ferrer-Conill from Karlstad University to understand emerging audience-oriented roles in newsrooms around the world (Ferrer-Conill & Tandoc, 2018). Jacob Nelson from Arizona State University and I also collaborated on a study that examined how one American newsroom's use of web analytics changed over time (Nelson & Tandoc, 2018). Here at NTU, I also collaborated with my colleagues Andrew Duffy and Rich Ling to observe newsrooms and interview journalists in Singapore to understand digital transformations, including web analytics use (Duffy, Ling, & Tandoc, 2017; Duffy, Tandoc, & Ling, 2017). I also became part of a project that involved Clarissa David and Evelyn Katigbak from the University of the Philippines and we examined how social media and web analytics have been embedded in online newsrooms in the Philippines (David, Tandoc, & Katigbak, 2016). Some interviews with Filipino journalists included in this book come from this project.

I have also been very fortunate to be able to work closely with excellent and hard-working students and supervisees, whose work and insights have helped me to discover new things about the intersection between web analytics and journalism. My PhD supervisee, Julian Maitra from the University of St. Gallen in Switzerland, brings into our collaborations his experience as a journalist, which involved dealing with social media metrics (Tandoc & Maitra, 2018). Here at NTU, my post-doctoral fellow, Shangyuan Wu, conducted interviews with online journalists in Hong Kong and Singapore to ask about their use of web analytics. Some of these interviews are also included in this book. My master's student Siti Rahil, a veteran journalist in Singapore, also completed her thesis on web analytics and interviewed 20 journalists across different news outlets in Singapore (Rahil, 2018). My master's student Lydia Teo also helped me in conducting a systematic review of the literature on web analytics and journalism. Julian and Lydia read earlier drafts of the book and provided me with great feedback.

Finally, I am extremely grateful to series editor Bob Franklin for his guidance throughout the writing of this book and, more importantly, for all the doors he has opened for me as a journalism researcher. I published my first journalism-related study with *Journalism Practice*, where Bob is the founding editor (Tandoc, Hellmueller, & Vos, 2013). I never imagined that I would be writing, or that I actually could write, a book—but here it is, thanks to Bob's mentorship and to his trust in my work.

It is through these previous experiences, my conversations with journalists around the world and my research collaborations as well as the insights from my students and teachers, my supervisees and mentors, that analytics is analyzed in this book.

## References


David, C., Tandoc, E., & Katigbak, E. (2016). *Social media embeddedness in the newsroom: Institutional arrangements and gatekeeping adjustments*. Paper presented at the International Communication Association, Fukuoka, Japan.

Duffy, A., Ling, R., & Tandoc, E. C. (2017). The people have spoken (the bastards?): Finding a legitimate place for feedback in the journalistic field. *Journalism Practice*, 1–18. doi:10.1080/17512786.2017.1372696

Duffy, A., Tandoc, E. C., & Ling, R. (2017). Frankenstein journalism. *Information, Communication & Society*, 1–15. doi:10.1080/1369118X.2017.1313884

Ferrer-Conill, R., & Tandoc, E. (2018). The audience-oriented editor: Making sense of the audience in the newsroom. *Digital Journalism, 6*(4), 436–453. doi:10.1080/21670811.2018.1440972

Hanusch, F., & Tandoc, E. (2017). Comments, analytics, and social media: The impact of audience feedback on journalists' market orientation. *Journalism*. doi:10.1177/1464884917720305

Jenner, M., & Tandoc, E. (2013). Newsrooms using Web metrics to evaluate staff, guide editorial decisions. *Reynolds Journalism Institute*. Retrieved from http://www.rjionline.org/blog/newsrooms-using-web-metrics-evaluate-staff-guide-editorial-decisions

Nelson, J. L., & Tandoc, E. (2018). Doing "well" or doing "good": What audience analytics reveal about journalism's competing goals. *Journalism Studies*, 1–17. doi:10.1080/1461670X.2018.1547122

Rahil, S. (2018). *Memes & the comedy of errors: How audience analytics is changing the news media in Singapore*. Paper presented at the International Communication Association Preconference on Audience Analytics, Prague.

Tandoc, E. (2013). *Web analytics, social media, and the journalistic doxa: The impact of audience feedback on the evolving gatekeeping process*

(PhD in Journalism), University of Missouri, Columbia, MO. Retrieved from https://bit.ly/2DBG1mr

Tandoc, E. (2014). Journalism is twerking? How web analytics is changing the process of gatekeeping. *New Media & Society, 16*(4), 559–575. doi:10.1177/1461444814530541

Tandoc, E. (2015). Why web analytics click: Factors affecting the ways journalists use audience metrics. *Journalism Studies, 16*(6), 782–799. doi:10.1080/1461670X.2014.946309

Tandoc, E., & Ferrucci, P. (2017). Giving in or giving up: What makes journalists use audience feedback in their news work? *Computers in Human Behavior, 68*, 149–156. doi:10.1016/j.chb.2016.11.027

Tandoc, E., Hellmueller, L., & Vos, T. P. (2013). Mind the gap: Between role conception and role enactment. *Journalism Practice, 7*(5), 539–554. doi:10.1080/17512786.2012.726503

Tandoc, E., & Maitra, J. (2018). News organizations' use of Native Videos on Facebook: Tweaking the journalistic field one algorithm change at a time. *New Media & Society, 20*(5), 1679–1696. doi:10.1177/1461444817702398

Tandoc, E., & Thomas, R. (2014). The ethics of web analytics: Implications of using audience metrics in news construction. *Digital Journalism, 3*(2), 243–258. doi:10.1080/21670811.2014.909122

# 1 Disrupting journalism

When I was still working as a reporter for the *Philippine Daily Inquirer*, the leading English broadsheet in the Philippines, I proposed to our research director a content analysis project that would involve analyzing articles and visuals on our front pages over the years and then comparing them with daily circulation rates. That was in 2008. I had just completed a master's degree, learned about content analysis as a research method, and become exposed to some basic statistical analyses. I thought it would be interesting and useful to explore which particular topics or newsmakers on the front page were associated with higher or lower circulation figures.

My idea was quickly rejected.

The reason was simple: The managing editor at that time told the research director that we did not want audience preferences influencing who or what we put on the front page. For a well-respected national newspaper, which takes pride in its editorial autonomy and agenda-setting power, this made perfect sense.

But things are different now.

Faced with shrinking audience sizes and declining advertising revenues, many news organizations around the world are adopting different tools to understand what it is that audiences want and what they do with news content. This has made web analytics a profitable business. Omniture, a company that offered products allowing clients to monitor how people use their websites, was purchased by Adobe, one of the world's leading software makers, for $1.8 billion in September 2009 (Johnson, 2009). *Web analytics*, which refers to processes and tools that systematically track, record, store, and analyze information about user characteristics, behavior, and patterns online, are now embedded in the routines of many newsrooms around the world, exposing journalists to a wealth of data they could never previously access (Lowrey & Woo, 2010; Petre, 2018; Vu, 2013).

Journalists no longer have to guess which stories audiences are reading—web analytics homepages display a website's top pages based on views in real time. "I mean, with print, we really don't have much idea how people are using it except for letters to the editor," a managing editor at a large American news organization in the Midwest told me in an interview in March 2013. "With digital, which is where we have three or more times more eyeballs everyday than we do in print, we know exactly what they're reading and for how long and where they're coming from."

News organizations have tracked information about their audiences in the past through readership surveys and broadcast ratings systems, but such information was limited, and therefore, the extent to which it affected news work was also restricted (Gans, 1979). But *audience metrics*—information about the characteristics and behavior of online audiences that are tracked, recorded, stored, and analyzed by web analytics tools—are different from survey results or broadcast ratings in a number of ways. Audience metrics are collected faster, often in real time; they are collected automatically, with audiences often unaware that their clicks and time spent on a page are being recorded; they are more inclusive, unlike surveys or ratings that come from only a subset of the actual audience; they are more comprehensive, providing journalists with a range of data; and they are also public, with news sites and social media platforms displaying news-related posts accompanied by popularity metrics (Lee & Tandoc, 2017). Since web analytics programs are usually prominently displayed in many newsrooms and are updated round the clock, they also provide journalists with easy and routine access to real-time audience data (Belair-Gagnon, 2018).

Such routine exposure to audience data has implications for how journalists carry out their work. Not sure if readers would like this article? Web analytics can supply the numbers. Would a photo go well with this story? Add it, and check if the numbers change. Not sure which headline is better? Test them, and see which one leads to more clicks. Web analytics has allowed journalists to confirm their news sense by quantifying their audiences. In many instances, this leads to journalists feeling good about themselves, especially when metrics support their editorial guesswork. Sometimes, journalists also get surprised when, after a couple of busy hours of editing stories, populating the site, and pushing out content on social media guided by analytics, they realize that on the homepage of their news site are articles about Taylor Swift, Justin Bieber, and Beyoncé.

It has also become commonplace for a few reporters to be introduced as the ones who bring in traffic, making some journalists proud but others jealous (Tandoc, 2014). Smaller media companies have even introduced a pay-per-click model (Fischer, 2014), while other newsrooms factor metrics into the performance evaluation of their employees (Tandoc & Jenner, 2016), such as in choosing the company's "employee of the month" (Belair-Gagnon, 2018). The increasing influence of the audience on news construction processes, facilitated by new information tools such as web analytics, is not only confined within online newsrooms. As many news organizations around the world integrate their traditional and digital platforms to cut production costs, there is some evidence that the impact of web analytics also spills over into decision-making for traditional platforms, such as for their print products (Nelson & Tandoc, 2018; Welbers, van Atteveldt, Kleinnijenhuis, Ruigrok, & Schaper, 2016).

## Why analytics clicks

In the not-so-distant past, journalists had the luxury, if not the excuse, to ignore audience feedback (Gans, 1979). But web analytics now makes it difficult for many journalists to do so, especially given the harsh economic realities that a lot of news organizations confront.

I remember speaking with a veteran journalist, then working as an assistant managing editor for online at a medium-sized American newsroom also in the Midwest, who remembered fondly how she witnessed the "heyday of journalism when the staff was twice as big and it felt like the public in general held journalism in higher regard." Things are different now, she told me in May 2013. "We're not dying. We're changing a lot. But I don't know whether journalism will ever regain the status it once had."

In the United States, newspapers have seen circulation rates decrease steadily in the last two decades—the slow increase in digital subscriptions has still not matched the sharp decreases in newspaper subscriptions (Barthel, 2018). Newspaper advertising revenues have also fallen from an estimated $49 billion in 2006 to $18 billion in 2016 (Barthel, 2018). It also doesn't help that many lists of the worst jobs in the United States include being a newspaper reporter, citing low pay and job stress (Doyle, 2018).

In the small but economically vibrant country of Singapore, online and social media platforms are now the most frequently used sources of news, way ahead of television and print newspapers (Tandoc, 2018). These changing consumption patterns come along with decreases in revenues for many news organizations, with Singapore Press Holdings, which publishes most newspapers in Singapore, including the paper-of-record *The Straits Times*, laying off 130 employees in October 2017 (Tandoc, 2018). In the Philippines, the Inquirer Holdings Incorporated, which owns *The Philippine Daily Inquirer*, where I worked previously, also saw its revenues drop from P39 million in 2010 to P24 million in 2013 (Tomacruz, 2017).

Faced with such economic uncertainties, journalism, said a former editor-in-chief of a prominent news organization in the United States that filed for bankruptcy in 2009, has no choice but to "either change or die."

One aspect of such change for legacy news organizations is adopting a digital-first mind-set. But digital journalism, compared with traditional forms of journalism, is a whole new world, where speed matters even more, sometimes at the expense of accuracy (Bruno, 2011); where journalistic outputs transcend spatial and temporal boundaries (Malik & Shapiro, 2017); where news distribution is no longer controlled by journalists (Tandoc & Vos, 2016); and where, a young reporter in the Philippines said in an interview in May 2015, journalists "get instant gratification—they know when their stories are being read or ignored." It is a realm where journalists no longer had the monopoly of setting the agenda as readers can share news stories or comment about or against them, potentially influencing how other readers subsequently attend to these news outputs. Going digital also led to quantifying the audience via analytics, which has made audiences more influential on news construction processes than before. Digital journalism widened traditional journalism's reach. But it also narrowed down its power.

## Where fields meet

While journalism considers its autonomy sacred, it has to live with its autonomy under constant attack. One of my favorite quotes about journalism comes from Patrick Champagne, who observed that:

> The history of journalism could well be in large part the story of an impossible autonomy—or, to put it in the least pessimistic way, the unending story of an autonomy that must be re-won because it is always threatened.
>
> (Champagne, 2005)

When I started my undergraduate studies in journalism in 1999, the *Philippine Daily Inquirer* was reeling from an advertising boycott mounted by friends of then President Joseph Estrada, who publicly announced his disdain for the newspaper's critical coverage of his administration. Some 18 years later, in July 2017, the family that owns the newspaper announced that it was selling its majority shares after earning the ire of President Rodrigo Duterte, who had publicly expressed his disdain for the newspaper's critical coverage of his administration's war on drugs.

Journalists are wary of political influence. Since journalism can influence public discourse and opinion, it is an attractive target for those seeking to amass political power. But the market is also a strong influence, especially because news organizations have become big businesses. While news does not make as much money as entertainment, owning a news organization provides legitimacy and political influence to media conglomerates (McChesney, 2013; McManus, 1994).

But that's not all.

While journalists have to protect their autonomy from politicians trying to influence their news coverage and from the business interests of their owners and advertisers, they are also now routinely exposed to the influence of their audiences who, through analytics, tell them what kinds of articles they like clicking on and spending time in. On top of that, they also need to consider the influence of technology platforms. Search engines like Google influence how high news sites appear when readers search for a term—this is important because search is an important source of site traffic (Dick, 2011). Social media platforms like Facebook also determine the reach of news—this is also important as social media referral is also a big source of site traffic (Bucher, 2012). It was no surprise to find that when Facebook announced it was tweaking its algorithm to prioritize native videos—or videos uploaded directly on Facebook as opposed to videos posted elsewhere—in the newsfeed, many news organizations subsequently increased their number of native videos on Facebook (Tandoc & Maitra, 2018).

News organizations and their journalists operate under layers and layers of influences, and web analytics is where many of these different influences meet.

It will be helpful to conceptualize journalism as a field, as French sociologist Pierre Bourdieu did, to understand its fragile position. Bourdieu (1998) observed that journalism as a field exerted influence on the political field, with politicians playing by journalism's rules to portray themselves to the public in particular ways, changing how they speak and behave when they are in front of the cameras. But journalism is equally vulnerable to the logics of the fields that surround it.

Its reliance on advertising as a business model has made journalism vulnerable to the influence of the economic field. Such an advertising model is also dependent on audience size. Indeed, gatekeeping theory, a theory of news selection, classifies the audience as a social-institutional influence that shapes journalistic outputs (Shoemaker & Vos, 2009).

Technologists also represent forces external to the journalistic field. In developing and introducing web analytics to journalism, the technological field is also introducing its own logic to journalism (Belair-Gagnon & Holton, 2018). This has potential to disrupt the journalistic field by changing its internal logic.

## Journalism disrupted

This book conceptualizes web analytics as an object of journalism where audiences, businesses, technologists, and journalists confront one another, negotiating the contours of online journalism in the process. Chapter 2 outlines the crucial role of audiences in journalism's evolution. As audiences become more fragmented and more autonomous (Napoli, 2011), their influence over journalism also increases, facilitated by new information systems, including web analytics. This is changing traditional news gatekeeping processes (Shoemaker & Vos, 2009). Chapter 3 locates the journalistic field alongside the political, economic, and technological fields. Financial and political pressures have long confronted journalism (Bourdieu, 1998). But the rising influence of technology across different industries is also disrupting traditional journalistic practices and norms. Web analytics was not originally developed for journalism. In entering the field of journalism, web analytics brings with it the logic of the technological field, confronting journalism's internal logic.

Chapter 4 examines how journalists adopt and adapt web analytics in their work. Studies argue that journalists tend to normalize technology, using new tools in a manner consistent with their old ways (Lasorsa, Lewis, & Holton, 2011; Singer, 2005). Some argue that this makes the field of journalism slow to change, always playing catch-up with the times, but others argue that this is a good thing as there's a good reason old ways of doing things persist (Lewis & Westlund, 2014; Thomas, 2016). But journalistic use of web analytics shows the processes of both journalists normalizing a new technology and negotiating new ways of news work (Tandoc, 2014). These patterns of use, ultimately, are what impacts on journalism. Chapter 5 problematizes how web analytics is disrupting, and in the process transforming, journalism as journalists balance the increasing influence of the audience on their work, the pressure exerted by the economic field, the logic imposed by the technological field, and the need to protect journalism's fragile autonomy.

Operating under layers of influences, journalists have long been engaging in a delicate balancing act. The metaphorical wall between a news organization's editorial and advertising departments speaks of the idealized divide between pursuing journalistic and business goals. That line seems to be vanishing as more and more newsrooms face increasing economic pressures (Artemas, Vos, & Duffy, 2018). This means that the balancing act becomes even more salient at the level of individual journalists, whose organizations now expect them to pursue both goals: Deliver good journalism as well as traffic.

The use of web analytics highlights this balancing act. Of course, journalists have long weighed what audiences want and what they need. But in the past, news judgment was all about balancing what one thinks audiences want and what one thinks audiences need. It was a process of reconciling one's own perceptions, often based on the journalist's own preferences and that of their peers, loved ones, and superiors (Gans, 1979). Now, while journalists remain as important arbiters of what information audiences need, they find themselves constantly comparing what they think audiences want with what audiences *actually* want. The numbers are there, flashed on the analytics screen, often located at the center of the newsroom, or on their office computers, sometimes even right on their mobile phones. This can be a source of pride, especially when one's hunches get affirmed subsequently by metrics. But this can also be a source of frustration for how does one balance audience wants and needs when the former is more measurable than the latter?

Newsrooms can now compare, based on metrics, a story with another story, a section with another section, and even a reporter with another reporter. This can motivate reporters to pursue popular stories and topics. This can also cause discord in the newsroom, especially when the stories of one section get promoted more often than those of the other (Neheli, 2018).

Studies have also found a shift in organizational culture as web analytics become routinized (Hanusch, 2017). For example, when I observed at three newsrooms in the United States in 2013, I noticed the use of the phrase "doing well" to describe particular stories during editorial meetings and interviews. A popular post would be described as something that "did very well." An argument to pursue a particular topic would be that the topic "has done well" in the past. Excitement over a planned story would include a comment predicting that it would "do well."

What does doing well mean?

It means getting good numbers. It means getting a lot of traffic. It means that old measures of whether or not a newspaper story did good—picked up by other media, got the attention of government officials, talked about by a lot of people, influenced policy, won an award—might be giving way to easily quantifiable assessments: Number of hits, page views, unique visitors, shares. When a colleague visited in 2016 one of the newsrooms that I had also visited in 2013, he also noticed the use of the phrase, although this time, it was often contrasted with "doing good," with many journalists at the newsroom conceding that doing well and doing good have become mutually exclusive goals (Nelson & Tandoc, 2018).

Web analytics is now embedded in news routines around the world, supplying editors and sometimes even reporters a steady stream of big data about the audience. Audience metrics have been used as the basis of subsequent newsroom decisions, including selecting which stories to display prominently on the homepage and deselecting stories to give way to new ones (Tandoc, 2014); deciding when to publish which story and on which platform (Duffy, Ling, & Tandoc, 2017; Hanusch, 2017); deciding to which topics to devote more coverage (Welbers et al., 2016); and assessing the performance of employees (Belair-Gagnon, 2018). Inquirer.net, the second most-read news site in the Philippines and the website of the *Philippine Daily Inquirer*, where I worked as a reporter before and where my proposal to compare front-page content and circulation figures was rejected, has also embraced web analytics. Online editors discuss the site's metrics during their weekly assessment meetings, using them to plan coverage and think of ways to better engage audiences.

Web analytics has disrupted the practice of journalism. It has helped to increase the influence of audiences on news construction processes. It has introduced the logic of the technological field into the field of journalism. It has instituted new practices, even realigning physical spaces of newsrooms, and constituted new, if not alternative, norms. Now that it has become deeply embedded in newsrooms, when it is now taken-for-granted, web analytics' impact on journalism is even more potent, which makes it important to keep track of how audience analytics is used and with what impact.

This book is about analyzing analytics.

## References

Artemas, K., Vos, T. P., & Duffy, M. (2018). Journalism hits a wall: Rhetorical construction of newspapers' editorial and advertising relationship. *Journalism Studies, 19*(7), 1004–1020. doi:10.1080/1461670X.2016.1249006

Barthel, M. (2018). Despite subscription surges for largest U.S. newspapers, circulation and revenue fall for industry overall. *Pew Research Center.* Retrieved from https://pewrsr.ch/2qFfi3q

Belair-Gagnon, V. (2018). News on the fly: Journalist-audience online engagement success as a cultural matching process. *Media, Culture & Society*. doi:10.1177/0163443718813473

Belair-Gagnon, V., & Holton, A. E. (2018). Boundary work, interloper media, and analytics in newsrooms. *Digital Journalism, 6*(4), 492–508. doi:10.1080/21670811.2018.1445001

Bourdieu, P. (1998). *On television*. New York: The New Press.

Bruno, N. (2011). Tweet first, verify later? How real-time information is changing the coverage of worldwide crisis events. *Reuters Institute for the Study of Journalism*. Retrieved from https://bit.ly/2Fuiztg

Bucher, T. (2012). Want to be on the top? Algorithmic power and the threat of invisibility on Facebook. *New Media & Society, 14*(7), 1164–1180. doi:10.1177/1461444812440159

Champagne, P. (2005). The "double dependency": The journalistic field between politics and markets. In R. Benson & E. Neveu (Eds.), *Bourdieu and the journalistic field* (pp. 48–64). Malden, MA: Polity Press.

Dick, M. (2011). Search engine optimisation in UK news production. *Journalism Practice, 5*(4), 462–477. doi:10.1080/17512786.2010.551020

Doyle, A. (2018). 12 Worst Jobs in America. *The Balance Careers*. Retrieved from https://bit.ly/2SoOEFq

Duffy, A., Ling, R., & Tandoc, E. C. (2017). The people have spoken (the bastards?): Finding a legitimate place for feedback in the journalistic field. *Journalism Practice*, 1–18. doi:10.1080/17512786.2017.1372696

Fischer, M. C. (2014). The pay-per-visit debate: Is chasing viral traffic hurting journalism? *American Journalism Review*. Retrieved from https://bit.ly/1i1pAvx

Gans, H. (1979). *Deciding what's news* (1st ed.). New York: Pantheon Books.

Hanusch, F. (2017). Web analytics and the functional differentiation of journalism cultures: Individual, organizational and platform-specific influences on newswork. *Information, Communication & Society, 20*(10), 1571–1586. doi: 10.1080/1369118X.2016.1241294

Johnson, B. (2009). Experts puzzled over Adobe's surprise purchase of Omniture. *The Guardian*. Retrieved from https://bit.ly/2MClGQB

Lasorsa, D. L., Lewis, S. C., & Holton, A. E. (2011). Normalizing twitter: Journalism practice in an emerging communication space. *Journalism Studies, 13*(1), 19–36. doi:10.1080/1461670x.2011.571825

Lee, E. J., & Tandoc, E. (2017). When news meets the audience: How audience feedback online affects news production and consumption. *Human Communication Research, 43*(4), 436–449. doi:10.1111/hcre.12123

Lewis, S. C., & Westlund, O. (2014). Actors, actants, audiences, and activities in cross-media news work. *Digital Journalism, 3*(1), 19–37. doi:10.1080/21670811.2014.927986

Lowrey, W., & Woo, C. W. (2010). The news organization in uncertain times: Business or institution? *Journalism and Mass Communication Quarterly, 87*(1), 41–61. doi:10.1177/107769901008700103

Malik, A., & Shapiro, I. (2017). What's digital? What's journalism? In B. Franklin & S. Eldridge II (Eds.), *The Routledge companion to digital journalism studies* (pp. 15–24). Milton Park, Abingdon: Routledge.

McChesney, R. W. (2013). *Digital disconnect: How capitalism is turning the internet against democracy.* New York: New Press.

McManus, J. (1994). *Market-driven journalism: Let the citizen beware?* Thousand Oaks, CA: Sage Publications.

Napoli, P. (2011). *Audience evolution: New technologies and the transformation of media audiences.* New York: Columbia University Press.

Neheli, N. B. (2018). News by numbers. *Digital Journalism, 6*(8), 1041–1051. doi:10.1080/21670811.2018.1504626

Nelson, J. L., & Tandoc, E. (2018). Doing "well" or doing "good": What audience analytics reveal about journalism's competing goals. *Journalism Studies,* 1–17. doi:10.1080/1461670X.2018.1547122

Petre, C. (2018). Engineering consent. *Digital Journalism, 6*(4), 509–527. doi:10.1080/21670811.2018.1444998

Shoemaker, P. J., & Vos, T. P. (2009). *Gatekeeping theory.* New York: Routledge.

Singer, J. (2005). The political j-blogger. *Journalism, 6*(2), 173–198. doi:10.1177/1464884905051009

Tandoc, E. (2014). Journalism is twerking? How web analytics is changing the process of gatekeeping. *New Media & Society, 16*(4), 559–575. doi:10.1177/1461444814530541

Tandoc, E. (2018). Singapore. *Reuters Institute Digital News Report.* Retrieved from https://bit.ly/2DEQrBQ

Tandoc, E., & Jenner, M. (2016). Analyzing web analytics: How newsrooms use web metrics in news construction and why. *Journal of Applied Journalism & Media Studies, 5*(3), 423–440. doi:10.1386/ajms.5.3.423_1

Tandoc, E., & Maitra, J. (2018). News organizations' use of Native Videos on Facebook: Tweaking the journalistic field one algorithm change at a time. *New Media & Society, 20*(5), 1679–1696. doi:10.1177/1461444817702398

Tandoc, E., & Vos, T. P. (2016). The journalist is marketing the news: Social media in the gatekeeping process. *Journalism Practice, 10*(8), 950–966. doi:10.1080/17512786.2015.1087811

Thomas, R. (2016). In defense of journalistic paternalism. *Journal of Media Ethics, 31*(2), 86–99. doi:10.1080/23736992.2016.1152895

Tomacruz, S. (2017). Fast facts: What you should know about the Inquirer group. *Rappler.* Retrieved from https://bit.ly/2KNely7

Vu, H. T. (2013). The online audience as gatekeeper: The influence of reader metrics on news editorial selection. *Journalism, 15*(8), 1094–1110. doi:10.1177/1464884913504259

Welbers, K., van Atteveldt, W., Kleinnijenhuis, J., Ruigrok, N., & Schaper, J. (2016). News selection criteria in the digital age: Professional norms versus online audience metrics. *Journalism, 17*(8), 1037–1053. doi:10.1177/1464884915595474

# 2 Changing audiences

When I asked a deputy digital editor at an online newsroom in the United States how important he thought the audience was, he said: "It's everything. If nobody's looking at the site, we're screwed." The newsroom, which publishes the city's main newspaper, had just undergone a physical transformation—the digital desk was placed right at the center, directly across the main entrance. The core of the newsroom consisted of two desks facing each other. This was where the managing editor for digital sat throughout the day. Surrounding her were the desks of the other sections—homepage, digital, metro, among others—arranged like a hexagon, so that the managing editor for digital, according to the deputy digital editor, "is at the center of the universe."

The deputy digital editor was tasked to edit and upload stories for the homepage. He was also tasked to push content on social media and keep an eye on the site's analytics. When I asked him what made him consider audience numbers to be important, his response was short and quick: "That's revenue. That's money."

Gatekeeping theory, a theory that seeks to explain and predict news selection, identifies the audience as one of the factors that can influence the news construction process (Shoemaker & Vos, 2009). First, it locates the audience at the social-institutional level of analysis, arguing that audiences can exert direct influences on news selection, such as by launching boycotts of media companies whose coverage they dislike, hitting those companies' bottom line. Second, gatekeeping also identifies the audience as an indirect influence on news content, as journalists make editorial decisions based on what they think audiences would be interested in. A journalist's orientation to the audience, which can affect how news is constructed, is an example of a routine-level influence (Shoemaker & Vos, 2009).

While early research on influences on news content argued that the audiences exerted a relatively weak influence on news work, especially when compared with other influences, such as journalists' personal characteristics or their relationship with news sources (Flegel & Chaffee, 1971; Gans, 1979; Gieber, 1960; Shoemaker & Reese, 1996; White, 1950), recent studies have demonstrated an increasing influence for the audience, especially with the use of web analytics. Through their clicks, likes, and shares, audiences are influencing not only individual journalists' decision-making considerations but also organizations' definition of key performance indicators. Furthermore, audiences now actively take part in news production and distribution. Armed with their mobile phones and connected to the internet, audiences can upload photographs or share information about newsworthy events they have witnessed personally, outside the control of journalists (Hermida, 2011).

The "people formerly known as the audience" are changing (Rosen, 2006).

## Rejecting audience feedback

Journalists used not to know very much about their audiences (Gans, 1979; Schlesinger, 1978; Wulfemeyer, 1984). In his observations in four newsrooms, Gans (1979) found that journalists had little knowledge of their actual audience. Often, journalists substituted their own preferences for those of their actual but "unknown" audience. Journalists also talked about an "invented audience" to justify editorial decisions (Gans, 1979).

Not knowing the actual audience also meant not knowing what the audience really wanted. For their news judgment, journalists relied instead on their "known" audience composed of family, superiors, and fellow journalists (Gans, 1979). This is plausibly an explanation for Baker's (2002, p. 96) assumption that "the media cannot be expected to provide the audience what it wants." Baker (2002) outlined several reasons for this, such as the public good nature of media products that results in low production as well as media monopoly that leads to low diversity in content. But another plausible reason at the micro-level is that media content producers did not really know what the audience wanted because, to begin with, they did not really know who their audience was (Gans, 1979).

Feedback used to come in the form of letters to the editors or phone calls to the newsroom—forms of feedback that had to be volunteered by a few members of the audience (Schlesinger, 1978). They were, however, considered unrepresentative of the actual audience. As years passed, and even with newer audience measurement systems such as readership surveys and television ratings, journalists still relied on their supervisors, their peers, their relatives, and their personal preferences (Beam, 1995; Sumpter, 2000). And even with internet technology that allowed user-generated contributions, journalists still paid scant attention to what the audience had to say. A study of the online community created by a news organization in Denmark found that journalists "thought citizen contributors did not have the standards and skills required for professional news production" (Bechmann, 2011, p. 25). The literature offers four plausible reasons for this institutional rejection of audience feedback (Tandoc, 2014):

1 **Many journalists dislike numbers and statistics**. This is the form audience research most often takes (Curtin & Maier, 2001; Gans, 1979). For example, readership surveys and broadcast ratings come in the form of statistics, offering information about audience size, and yet some journalists did not consider them useful at all (Beam, 1995; Schlesinger, 1978).
2 **Journalists and audiences have divergent preferences**. Comparisons of the story preferences of journalists and their audiences yielded contrasting results. One study asked 40 newspaper subscribers and 13 journalists to rank a list of stories by preference, finding substantial agreement between the news preferences of journalists and subscribers (Atwood, 1970). Similarly, a survey of 65 editors of Wisconsin daily newspapers and 402 Wisconsin residents found that editors' opinions about a political protest were largely similar to and somewhat influenced by those of the public (Martin, O'Keefe, & Nayman, 1972). However, a survey of 20 television journalists and 250 viewers found divergent preferences (Wulfemeyer, 1984). The journalists thought that their viewers were more interested in sex, crime, and violence; the viewers reported that they were more interested in economy, consumerism, and education (Wulfemeyer, 1984). Despite this inconsistency in earlier studies, recent studies of online news agree on the divergence in the preferences of journalists and audiences, with journalists preferring public affairs stories, and audiences viewing and sharing sports and entertainment stories the most (Boczkowski, 2010; Boczkowski, Mitchelstein, & Walter, 2011; Thorson, 2008). A cross-national study of news content, journalists, and audiences also found that while audiences from different countries tend to agree on what is newsworthy, their preferences for certain types of topical coverage often disagree with what the news media publish (Shoemaker & Cohen, 2006).

3 **Many journalists have a pejorative view of the audience**. A survey of 489 editors and reporters across ten newsrooms in 1981 found that journalists tend to have a "patronizing and unflattering view" of the audience, overestimating the audience's preference for superficial materials and underestimating preference for important content (Atkin, Burgoon, & Burgoon, 1983, p. 51). Though audience feedback also came not only in the form of cold statistics but also in conversations and interactions with some members of the audience, such as phone calls and letters to the editor, many journalists dismissed this feedback as coming from "cranks" and "idiosyncratic" members of the audience (Schlesinger, 1978). These forms of feedback were therefore not trusted and considered not representative of the actual audience.

4 **Journalists value and protect their autonomy**. Beam (1995) found that many journalists believed that incorporating results of readership surveys in editorial operations might erode journalistic quality. So, what journalists did not know about the audience they filled with their own notion of professionalism by relying on traditional news standards that guide news content (Schlesinger, 1978).

## Defining the "audience"

Understanding journalists' perceptions of, and their relationship with, their audiences requires understanding who the audience is. The term *audience* is often defined based on its empirical components. For example, Ang (1991, p. 33) said a common way of defining it was: "a collection of spectators; a group of individuals gathered together to attend to a performance and 'receive' a message 'sent' by another." This definition is consistent with an unflattering view of a passive receiver (McQuail, 2010) that has given rise to conceptualizations of the audience as mere recipients of media messages or products to be sold to advertisers (Loosen & Schmidt, 2012; Webster & Phalen, 1994).

The audience is an institutional construction (Bermejo, 2007; Ettema & Whitney, 1994; Napoli, 2011; Sullivan, 2013; Turow, 2005). How it is defined is based on social and institutional contexts. The audience "is always closely connected to the ways in which the audience is defined and by whom" (Sullivan, 2013, p. 16). Specifically, Napoli (2011, p. 3) said that the "institutionalized audience" is "socially constructed by media industries, advertisers, and associated audience measurement firms." Answering why the audience has been conceived of as passive receivers of information should lead us back to how the news media have come to this institutional abstraction of the audience as a passive and an unthinking mass, specifically the ways the news media have measured their audiences before. These traditional audience measurement techniques include:

**Circulation rates**. Newspaper companies monitor their average number of distributed copies in a predefined time period, such as day or month (National Readership Survey, 2017). Since some copies are offered for free, circulation rates do not automatically correspond to the number of sold copies. They also do not account for pass-on readership, or when someone who paid for a copy shares the same copy with other readers.

**Readership surveys**. News companies commission their own or subscribe to polling companies who interview face-to-face or via telephone a sample of users or households to ask about their media use habits. Surveys measure, at most, exposure or recall of particular brands. Results also come from a subset of the actual audience.

**Broadcast ratings**. News companies also subscribe to audience measurement firms who track broadcast media use using a combination of peoplemeters and user diaries. Peoplemeters are box-like recording devices connected to TV receivers of randomly selected households, where each family member is required to push a different remote-control button when switching the TV on. This records the viewing patterns of individual household members. Some companies also ask household members to record a diary of their media use (Webster, Phalen, & Lichty, 2006).

These traditional audience measurement techniques aggregated individual responses to understand general patterns of media use (Ang, 1991; Schlesinger, 1978). However, the process of aggregation leads to depersonalization (Ang, 1991). Reduced into numbers and detached from their personal contexts, members of the audience have been easily perceived as objects of management or manipulation by the media (McQuail, 2010). For example, television ratings are used as a form of currency for financial transactions between the media and their advertisers, instead of a measure of social behavior (Sullivan, 2013). Similarly, scholarly definitions are also mostly dictated by commercial considerations (Bermejo, 2007).

Understanding how the news media quantify their audiences is important because how the industry measures the audience can influence how much influence the audience exerts on news construction. For example, Ettema and Whitney (1994) argued that "the measurement of audience behavior, not audience behavior *per se*, changes the media" (p. 78). The imagined audience, not the actual audience, influences news outputs (de Sola Pool & Shulman, 1959). For example, Hardin (2005) found that sports editors selected content based on their own perceptions of what would interest the audience rather than the actual audience itself. A survey of health journalists also found that how health journalists conceive of their audiences influenced even the writing and argumentation techniques they employed in their stories (Hinnant, Len-Ríos, & Oh, 2011).

But while the conceptualization of a passive, mass audience might have served traditional media institutions well, it no longer accurately reflects how much the audience has evolved. The audience is no longer composed of passive media consumers. Individuals, or whom Bruns (2003) called *produsers*, now consume and produce messages at the same time. Napoli (2011) outlined two important changes that challenge the traditional conceptualizations of the audience: Audience fragmentation and audience autonomy.

**Audience fragmentation** refers to the disintegration of the mass audience, as abundant and diverse media choices have fragmented audiences (Napoli, 2011). This phenomenon challenges the traditional exposure-based approach of understanding the audience. Old audience measurement systems, such as readership surveys, just counted how many individuals were exposed to a particular content, when exposure is not a good predictor of audience behavior (Potter, 2009). Furthermore, exposure-based audience measurement techniques are no longer adequate in an information-saturated context. For example, readership surveys are skewed in favor of legacy media that have better name-recall among newspaper readers, when these viewers attend to other sources of similar content they cannot easily remember but they can easily search on Google (Napoli, 2011).

**Audience autonomy** refers to the increasing control that the audience now enjoys with respect to media content, allowing new ways of interaction with content, such as "increased capacity for user-generated content" (Napoli, 2011, p. 8). This comes in the form of interactivity afforded by the internet, or even the ability to skip advertisements in television programs recorded in one's DVR (Napoli, 2011). This phenomenon also has implications on audience measurement. Traditional techniques tend to only account for exposure, contributing to a conceptualization of a passive audience. But audiences now engage with content in different ways, from viewing it across different platforms, sharing it, or even commenting on it.

## Audiences in journalism

These patterns in audience evolution are also seen in how news audiences are changing. News organizations no longer have the monopoly of news production and delivery, as non-journalists are also now engaging in journalistic actions. An increasing number of news audiences get their news primarily from non-news platforms, such as social media sites, and often also incidentally. This changes not only how news audiences get their news, contributing to fragmentation. Now that news audiences can decide when to attend to what types of news and in which platform, as well as what to do with the news they consume, consistent with audience autonomy, it also changes how audiences process and value news. For example, some of the research that my colleagues and I have been doing at Nanyang Technological University in Singapore shows that news is increasingly being valued more for its social utility than for its informational use—that is, news is considered a social currency that social media users exchange to maintain their friendship, more than an accurate representation of a socially important issue or event. Audience fragmentation and autonomy are also changing the relationship between journalists and audiences.

From letters sent and phone calls made to newspaper and television newsrooms in the older days (Gans, 1979; Schlesinger, 1978), audience participation in the news construction process now comes in the form of comments that appear after each online story (Braun & Gillespie, 2011), posts in social media such as Twitter and Facebook (Hermida, 2010, 2012; Hermida, Fletcher, Korell, & Logan, 2012), and real-time metrics through web analytics (Lee, Lewis, & Powers, 2012; MacGregor, 2007). Studies on the changing interaction between audiences and journalists show three major patterns of how audiences now figure in the journalistic news construction process (Tandoc & Vos, 2016).

First, news audiences have provided journalists with leads, commentaries, reviews, photos, videos, or even stories, which I will refer to as **content contribution**. This is different from online users functioning as the originators of content who function outside the gates controlled by journalists. Crowdsourcing, which refers to the process of obtaining ideas, pieces of information, or details from people, has become popular in newsrooms around the world (Akagi & Linning, 2013; Poell & Borra, 2012). Scholars also referred to user-generated content (Harrison, 2009; Singer & Ashman, 2009; Wardle & Williams, 2010; Williams, Wardle, & Wahl-Jorgensen, 2010), something that has been embraced by news media giants such as CNN and BBC that encourage and devote web pages to contributions from the audience, such as photos and videos. Comments are also considered content contributions from the audience (Singer & Ashman, 2009), and while user comments range from serious to hilarious, sometimes even resorting to personal attacks (Braun & Gillespie, 2011), a growing number of people consider reading readers' comments to be amusing and entertaining, so that reader comments themselves also draw in more readers. But while collecting content from audiences can be looked at as free labor, journalists have to balance this with their traditional norms. "Journalists may worry that amateur-quality contributions from users will undercut the professional sheen of their own work; news organizations may find they must work harder to protect their brand as they incorporate user-generated content" (Braun & Gillespie, 2011, p. 384).

Second, audiences have become key players in **content dissemination**. For example, automated lists of most popular stories have become standard elements in most news websites (Thorson, 2008). Similarly, many news sites also prominently display sharing features that allow users to share a story through their social media accounts, such as on Twitter and Facebook (Hermida et al., 2012). These website features have become forms of recommendation that other users employ as heuristics to decide which content to access (Thorson, 2008). Thus, Hermida and colleagues (2012, p. 821) argued that "the traditional gatekeeping function of the media is weakened as a significant proportion of news consumers turn to family, friends, and acquaintances to alert them to items of interest." When users share particular articles they like, they also facilitate the audience channel through which these media content will reach other members of the audience (Shoemaker & Vos, 2009). Twitter is considered particularly suited to breaking news stories (Hermida, 2010; Jewitt, 2009) as shown in a string of international events first broken into a large audience through tweets from ordinary citizens who happened to be on the scene at that moment (Jewitt, 2009). But while audiences take part in distributing news content through their social media accounts and their emails, these audience activities actually pose threats to established media, which now find these interactions operating outside their websites and in third-party applications that take audience attention and subsequently advertising revenues away from news sites (Hermida, 2012).

Third, audiences have become more influential through **content customization**. While audiences exert direct influences on what is uploaded online by uploading pieces of information themselves, audience preferences, communicated through new forms of feedback and quantified using new audience measurement systems, also exert indirect influences on journalistic decisions. This is where web analytics becomes central. Web analytics can inform newsrooms which stories are attracting a large number of clicks, the origins of these clicks in terms of actual physical location and in terms of referrals online, and what readers do with the contents they access (e.g. share a story on social media, email it to a friend, etc.). Access to these metrics equips journalists with information on audience preferences that newsrooms might use to guide editorial decisions to target particular audiences. With web analytics, newsrooms can customize content to fit audience preferences, such as by rewriting headlines, updating stories, adding visual elements, and pursuing trending topics.

New information and communication technologies have helped to increase the influence of audiences on the news construction process. News audiences have long been quantified. Circulation figures, readership surveys, and broadcast ratings provided news organizations a quantified understanding of audience preferences and behavior. But as these preferences and behaviors changed with the rise of digital technologies that allowed audiences to not only consume but also distribute and produce content, web analytics has helped newsrooms to catch up in understanding audiences online. In doing so, web analytics systems are also facilitating the changing power dynamics between journalists and audiences by making complex audience preferences and online behaviors accessible and quantifiable.

Web analytics helps news organizations to keep pace with the challenges to audience measurement brought by audience fragmentation and autonomy. As more and more news audiences get their news from social media platforms, web analytics helps news organizations to keep track of how their content is distributed on social media. Web analytics also allows news organizations to quantify different forms of audience interaction with particular news content and their news site in general beyond just mere exposure. In doing so, web analytics contributes not only to the evolution of the audience, but also to the changing relationship between journalists and audiences.

## References

Akagi, K., & Linning, S. (2013). Crowdsourcing done right. *Between the spreadsheets*. Retrieved from cjr.org website: http://www.cjr.org/between_the_spreadsheets/crowdsourcing_done_right.php

Ang, I. (1991). *Desperately seeking the audience*. New York: Routledge.

Atkin, C. K., Burgoon, J. K., & Burgoon, M. (1983). How journalists perceive the reading audience. *Newspaper Research Journal, 4*(2), 51–63.

Atwood, L. E. (1970). How newsmen and readers perceive each others' story preferences. *Journalism & Mass Communication Quarterly, 47*(2), 296–302. doi:10.1177/107769907004700210

Baker, C. E. (2002). *Media, markets, and democracy.* New York: Cambridge University Press.

Beam, R. A. (1995). How newspapers use readership research. *Newspaper Research Journal, 16*(2), 28–38. doi:10.1177/073953299501600204

Bechmann, A. (2011). Closer apart? The networks of cross-media news production. In D. Domingo & C. Paterson (Eds.), *Making online news* (Vol. 2). New York: Peter Lang Publishing Inc.

Bermejo, F. (2007). *The internet audience: Constitution and measurement.* New York: Peter Lang Publishing Inc.

Boczkowski, P. J. (2010). The divergent online news preferences of journalists and readers. *Communications of the ACM, 53*(11), 24–26. doi:10.1145/1839676.1839685

Boczkowski, P. J., Mitchelstein, E., & Walter, M. (2011). Convergence across divergence: Understanding the gap in the online news choices of journalists and consumers in Western Europe and Latin America. *Communication Research, 38*(3), 376–396. doi:10.1177/0093650210384989

Braun, J., & Gillespie, T. (2011). Hosting the public discourse, hosting the public: When online news and social media converge. *Journalism Practice, 5*(4), 383–398. doi:10.1080/17512786.2011.557560

Bruns, A. (2003). Gatewatching, not gatekeeping: Collaborative online news. *Media International Australia Incorporating Culture & Policy, 107*(1), 31–44.

Curtin, P. A., & Maier, S. R. (2001). Numbers in the newsroom: A qualitative examination of a quantitative challenge. *Journalism and Mass Communication Quarterly, 78*(4), 720–738.

de Sola Pool, I., & Shulman, I. (1959). Newsmen's fantasies, audiences, and newswriting. *The Public Opinion Quarterly, 23*(2), 145–158.

Ettema, J., & Whitney, D. C. (1994). The money arrow: An introduction to audiencemaking. In J. Ettema & D. C. Whitney (Eds.), *Audiencemaking: How the media create the audience* (pp. 1–18). New York: Sage.

Flegel, R. C., & Chaffee, S. H. (1971). Influences of editors, readers, and personal opinions on reporters. *Journalism & Mass Communication Quarterly, 48*(4), 645–651. doi:10.1177/107769907104800404

Gans, H. (1979). *Deciding what's news* (1st ed.). New York: Pantheon Books.

Gieber, W. (1960). How the "gatekeepers" view local civil liberties news. *Journalism Quarterly, 37*(2), 199–205. doi:10.1177/107769906003700204

Hardin, M. (2005). Stopped at the gate: Women's sports, "reader interest," and decision making by editors. *Journalism and Mass Communication Quarterly, 82*(1), 62.

Harrison, J. (2009). User-generated content and gatekeeping at the BBC hub. *Journalism Studies, 11*(2), 243–256. doi:10.1080/14616700903290593

Hermida, A. (2010). Twittering the news. *Journalism Practice, 4*(3), 297–308. doi:10.1080/17512781003640703

Hermida, A. (2011). Fluid spaces, fluid journalism: The role of the "active recipient" in participatory journalism. In J. Singer, A. Hermida, D. Domingo, A. Heinonen, S. Paulussen, T. Quandt, Z. Reich, & M. Vujnovic (Eds.), *Participatory journalism: Guarding open gates at online newspapers* (pp. 177–191). Malden, MA: John Wiley & Sons.

Hermida, A. (2012). Social journalism: Exploring how social media is shaping journalism. In E. Siapera & A. Veglis (Eds.), *The handbook of global online journalism* (pp. 309–328). Malden, MA: John Wiley & Sons, Inc.

Hermida, A., Fletcher, F., Korell, D., & Logan, D. (2012). Share, like, recommend. *Journalism Studies, 13*(5–6), 815–824. doi:10.1080/1461670x.2012.664430

Hinnant, A., Len-Ríos, M. E., & Oh, H. J. (2011). Are health journalists' practices tied to their perceptions of audience? An attribution and expectancy-value approach. *Health Communication, 27*(3), 234–243. doi:10.1080/10410236.2011.578331

Jewitt, R. (2009). The trouble with twittering: Integrating social media into mainstream news. *International Journal of Media & Cultural Politics, 5*(3), 233–246. doi:10.1386/macp.5.3.233_3

Lee, A. M., Lewis, S. C., & Powers, M. (2012). Audience clicks and news placement: A study of time-lagged influence in online journalism. *Communication Research*. doi:10.1177/0093650212467031

Loosen, W., & Schmidt, J.-H. (2012). (Re-)discovering the audience. *Information, Communication & Society, 15*(6), 867–887. doi:10.1080/1369118x.2012.665467

MacGregor, P. (2007). Tracking the online audience. *Journalism Studies, 8*(2), 280–298. doi:10.1080/14616700601148879

Martin, R. K., O'Keefe, G. J., & Nayman, O. B. (1972). Opinion agreement and accuracy between editors and their readers. *Journalism & Mass Communication Quarterly, 49*(3), 460–468. doi:10.1177/107769907204900305

McQuail, D. (2010). *Mass communication theory*. Thousand Oaks, CA: SAGE.

Napoli, P. (2011). *Audience evolution: New technologies and the transformation of media audiences*. New York: Columbia University Press.

National Readership Survey. (2017). *What's the difference between readership and circulation?* Retrieved from http://www.nrs.co.uk/nrs-print/readership-and-circulation-trends/readership-vs-circulation/

Poell, T., & Borra, E. (2012). Twitter, YouTube, and Flickr as platforms of alternative journalism: The social media account of the 2010 Toronto G20 protests. *Journalism, 13*(6), 695–713. doi:10.1177/1464884911431533

Potter, W. J. (2009). Conceptualizing the audience. In R. Nabi & M. B. Oliver (Eds.), *The SAGE handbook of media processes and effects* (pp. 19–34). Thousand Oaks, CA: Sage.

Rosen, J. (2006). The people formerly known as the audience. *Huffington Post*. Retrieved from Huffington Post website: http://www.huffingtonpost.com/jay-rosen/the-people-formerly-known_1_b_24113.html

Schlesinger, P. (1978). *Putting 'reality' together.* Beverly Hills, CA: Sage.

Shoemaker, P. J., & Cohen, A. (2006). *News around the world: Content, practitioners, and the public.* New York: Routledge.

Shoemaker, P. J., & Reese, S. D. (1996). *Mediating the message: Theories of influences on mass media content* (2nd ed.). White Plains, NY: Longman.

Shoemaker, P. J., & Vos, T. P. (2009). *Gatekeeping theory.* New York: Routledge.

Singer, J., & Ashman, I. (2009). "Comment is free, but facts are sacred": User-generated content and ethical constructs at the Guardian. *Journal of Mass Media Ethics, 24*(1), 3–21. doi:10.1080/08900520802644345

Sullivan, J. (2013). *Media audiences: Effects, users, institutions, and power.* Thousand Oaks, CA: Sage.

Sumpter, R. S. (2000). Daily newspaper editors' audience construction routines: A case study. *Critical Studies in Media Communication, 17*(3), 334–346. doi:10.1080/15295030009388399

Tandoc, E. (2014). Journalism is twerking? How web analytics is changing the process of gatekeeping. *New Media & Society, 16*(4), 559–575. doi:10.1177/1461444814530541

Tandoc, E., & Vos, T. P. (2016). The journalist is marketing the news: Social media in the gatekeeping process. *Journalism Practice, 10*(8), 950–966. doi: 10.1080/17512786.2015.1087811

Thorson, E. (2008). Changing patterns of news consumption and participation. *Information, Communication and Society, 11*(4), 473–489. doi:10.1080/13691180801999027

Turow, J. (2005). Audience construction and culture production: Marketing surveillance in the digital age. *Annals of the American Academy of Political and Social Science, 597*, 103–121.

Wardle, C., & Williams, A. (2010). Beyond user-generated content: a production study examining the ways in which UGC is used at the BBC. *Media, Culture & Society, 32*(5), 781–799. doi:10.1177/0163443710373953

Webster, J., & Phalen, P. (1994). Victim, consumer, or commodity? Audience models in communication policy. In J. Ettema & D. C. Whitney (Eds.), *Audiencemaking: How the media create the audience* (pp. 19–37). New York: Sage.

Webster, J., Phalen, P., & Lichty, L. (2006). *Ratings analysis: The theory and practice of audience research.* Mahwah, NJ: Lawrence Earlbaum Associates.

White, D. M. (1950). The 'gatekeeper.' A case study in the selection of news. *Journalism Quarterly, 27*, 383–390.

Williams, A., Wardle, C., & Wahl-Jorgensen, K. (2010). "Have they got news for us?" Audience revolution or business as usual at the BBC? *Journalism Practice, 5*(1), 85–99. doi:10.1080/17512781003670031

Wulfemeyer, K. T. (1984). Perceptions of viewer interests by local TV journalists. *Journalism Quarterly, 61*(2), 432–435. doi:10.1177/107769908406100231

# 3 Overlapping fields

The web analytics ecosystem brings together different actors. First, there are software developers designing the system and company staffers marketing these tools to clients. Second, there are those buying the tools—in journalism, this tends to be the owner of the news organization or the head of marketing. Third, once an analytics tool is purchased and deployed in the newsroom, there are those actually using it by tracking audience metrics; making sense of the data; compiling reports; and providing short- and long-term recommendations to their newsrooms on a regular, sometimes day-to-day, basis, potentially shaping crucial editorial decisions.

In some newsrooms, none of these actors would be journalists—at least not in the traditional sense.

While in many newsrooms, analytics tools are monitored by editors on a day-to-day basis, some newsrooms hire third-party companies to track their metrics and compile reports for them. In some smaller newsrooms, web analytics is handled by their marketing departments, which provide weekly or monthly briefings to the newsroom. Other newsrooms hire a web analytics manager, who is more a technology expert than a journalist.

Frustrated that some important stories are not covered by his newsroom because these stories would not get good audience numbers, a desk editor for an online-only newsroom in Hong Kong blamed, among other things, his newsroom's "technical team who are only looking at the figures; they do not have a journalism background, they just look at the figures—page views, duration, something like that."

Web analytics tools were not originally designed for journalism. Marketing professionals, not journalists, were among the earliest commercial users of web analytics. Now embedded in many newsrooms around the world, web analytics represents the intersection of journalists, businesspeople, and technologists. It represents the confrontation between the fields of journalism, business, and technology.

## Journalism as a field

Gatekeeping theory's explanation of how news gets selected is both simple and complex. On the one hand, its basic assumption is simple: Gatekeeping is the process through which bits and pieces of information become news by passing through several gates controlled by gatekeepers who can open or close the gates, shaping and reshaping the information along the way. On the other hand, this process and its stages operate under several layers of influence, ranging from the gatekeeper's personal traits, news routines, the news organization, social actors external to journalism, to the larger social system (Herman & Chomsky, 2002; Shoemaker & Reese, 1996; Shoemaker & Vos, 2009). Because of this complexity, many gatekeeping studies focus on just one level of analysis, in effect studying the news construction process in segments.

The framework of field theory can help to provide a more holistic analysis of this multi-layered gatekeeping process (Benson, 2004; Russell, 2007). Field theory seeks to study the journalistic field as a whole by accounting for not only the relationships between agents within the field but also the relationship of the journalistic field as a whole with other fields that might also be exerting influence on journalism (Benson & Neveu, 2005; Siapera & Spyridou, 2012).

Field theory originated in the field of physical sciences but was adapted into journalism through the work of French sociologist Pierre Bourdieu and the researchers who built on his theoretical work (Benson & Neveu, 2005; Neveu, 2007). The framework of field theory builds on four key concepts: *Field, capital, doxa*, and *habitus*. The concept of a field has been used in numerous studies, conceptualizing as fields social domains such as politics, the arts (Bourdieu, 2005), organizations (Emirbayer & Johnson, 2008), sports (Stempel, 2005), and journalism (Benson, 2006; Bourdieu, 1998, 2005; Handley & Rutigliano, 2012). A field refers to a "field of forces," which agents struggle to either transform or preserve (Bourdieu, 1985, 2005). The journalistic field is an example, although journalism is often considered part of the more encompassing field of cultural production (Benson, 2006; Siapera & Spyridou, 2012). The journalistic field, Bourdieu (1998, p. 39) said, is a "microcosm with its own laws, defined by its own position in the world at large and by the attractions and repulsions to which it is subject from other such microcosms."

To exist in a field "is to differentiate oneself" (Bourdieu, 2005, p. 39). A field differentiates itself from other fields through a system of rules. This is called the doxa, which refers to a "'universe of tacit presuppositions' that organize action within the field" (Benson & Neveu, 2005, p. 3). For example, when journalists join the field, they accept and subsequently play by particular conventions as part of the job. News values, which refer to an enduring set of criteria of what makes something newsworthy, are examples of journalistic doxa (Willig, 2013). Other principles that govern the practice of journalism, such as the problematic norm of objectivity or the normative idea of providing what the audience needs, are also examples of journalistic doxa.

Norms dominate and persist as agents in the field perpetuate them. These agents within the journalistic field participate in a struggle to either transform or preserve the field, but they do so within the field's internal rules.

These agents are shaped by, and bring with them, their respective habitus, which refers to dispositions accumulated through an agent's experience over time that generate "practices and perceptions" (Johnson, 1993, p. 5). The habitus "implies understanding the journalistic game" which allows an individual to understand and play by the rules (Willig, 2013, p. 8). The habitus also refers to an agent's historical trajectory within the field, which is based on personal and professional experiences accumulated from various social positions. Such collection of experiences produces particular sets of knowledge and ways of understanding the game.

The framework of field theory is focused on both the field, with its own doxa, in relation to other fields and the agents within the field, each with their habitus, in relation to one another. For example, Bourdieu (1998) argued that the field of television had amassed enough meta-capital (see Couldry, 2003) to be able to exert influences on other fields, such as the political field, thereby transforming the struggles within these other fields. In the same vein, the journalistic field also finds itself influenced by the other fields around it, such as the political and the economic fields that constantly challenge its already fragile autonomy. These external pressures influence how agents within the journalistic field participate in the struggle to either preserve or transform the field.

The concept of capital refers to "the specific forms of agency and prestige within a given field" (Sterne, 2003, p. 375). It refers to various forms of resources, some more dominant than the others, but each being convertible into the other forms, depending on an agent's relative position within the field. These forms of capital enable agents to participate in the struggle (Handley & Rutigliano, 2012), differentiating one agent from the other in terms of relative power based on accumulated capital. Thus, capital is also something that agents seek. Field theory refers to two main forms of capital: Economic and cultural (Benson, 2006; Benson & Neveu, 2005), but field theory scholars also refer to social and symbolic capital (Sallaz & Zavisca, 2007; Willig, 2013).

Economic capital refers to money or assets transformable into money (Benson, 2006). It is considered as the dominant capital in most fields. In journalism studies, it has been operationalized in terms of advertising revenues, circulation rates, television ratings, and audience size (Benson, 2004, 2006; Benson & Neveu, 2005; Siapera & Spyridou, 2012). Cultural capital refers to possession of competence in a socially valued area (Sallaz & Zavisca, 2007), often operationalized as possession of journalistic excellence or quality as conferred by professional or academic groups, such as the Pulitzer Prize in the US (Benson, 2006; Benson & Neveu, 2005). However, other scholars have defined it in terms of accumulated knowledge that can come in embodied, objectified, or institutionalized forms (Bourdieu, 1986; Siapera & Spyridou, 2012). Skills and educational credentials of online journalists, for example, have been used to assess the cultural capital of the online journalistic field (Siapera & Spyridou, 2012).

Since they are the basic currencies that agents use in their struggles within the field, forms of capital are also used to amass more capital and elevate one's position in the field. For example, news organizations call attention to the awards they win, a form of symbolic capital, to attract more readers and increase circulation and advertising figures, which are forms of economic capital. News organizations also use their economic capital to invest in investigative pieces with the hopes of gaining recognition from the field. Benson and Neveu (2005, p. 4) argued: "Organizations who dominate the field are those successful in converting one form of capital into the other."

The question of autonomy is central to field theory. Fields are always confronted with oppositions between the heteronomous and the autonomous poles (Neveu, 2007). While cultural capital brings the field closer to its autonomous pole, distinguishing it from other fields, thereby protecting its autonomy, economic capital brings the field closer to its heteronomous pole, making it vulnerable to external forces. With its dependence on advertising to survive, the journalistic field has been characterized as having a high degree of heteronomy (Bourdieu, 2005). This can be seen in many studies and critiques that have outlined the ways economic considerations influence journalism. While some studies have focused on the dangers of state control of the press (Gans, 2003), other scholars have also pointed out the equally dangerous influence business pressures can exert on journalism and, consequently, on the public discourse it shapes (McChesney, 2013;

McManus, 1994). The once sacred metaphorical wall between editorial and advertising within newsrooms is emblematic of this concern. It was supposed to keep newsrooms autonomous from any pressure to please or protect advertisers.

Field theory's focus on autonomy also provides a framework to conceptualize emerging players in the journalistic field, even those coming from non-journalism backgrounds. It speaks of new entrants to the field, who can have the power to either destabilize or preserve the field (Benson, 1999; Tandoc & Jenkins, 2017). While new entrants are confronted by journalism's internal rules, new entrants to the field also bring with them not only their own habitus but also the internal doxa of their own fields. In introducing web analytics into individual newsrooms, technologists are also introducing into the journalistic field the peculiar logic of the technological field.

## The business of analytics

Web analytics refers to "the measurement, collection, analysis and reporting of Internet data for the purposes of understanding and optimizing Web usage" (DAA, 2008). It is "a way of learning how users interact with websites and mobile apps by automatically recording aspects of users' behavior and then combining and transforming the behavior into data that can be analyzed" (Beasley, 2013, p. 2). In journalism studies, others have used the terms "editorial analytics" (Cherubini & Nielsen, 2016), "newsroom analytics" (Petre, 2018), and "audience analytics" (Zamith, 2018). These terms refer to larger systems: While web analytics refers to the collection and use of data from websites, newsrooms can also collect metrics from audiences outside web spaces to complement what they get from web analytics. For example, Zamith (2018, p. 418) defines audience analytics as "systems that capture a range of audience behaviors." Newsroom and editorial analytics refer to a collection of systems and tools that provide users with a host of information not only about audience behavior but also about publishing patterns and performance of competitors that might not always be about the audience. Thus, editorial analytics also include offline audience metrics, such as audience survey results, that complement web analytics to provide newsrooms with a more holistic sense of their performance vis-à-vis their competitors. Web analytics, then, refers to a specific type of audience measurement online. A more specific type of web analytics is *social media analytics*, which refers to processes and tools that capture data on audience behaviors and patterns specifically from social media sites and platforms.

Numerous web analytics tools are now available, some even catered specifically, to news organizations. Now embedded in many newsrooms around the world, web analytics have become objects of journalism, and the technologists who created them, the business managers marketing them to journalists, and the audience engagement managers using them have become important agents, comprising new entrants, to the journalistic field. While most of these analytics tools are expensive, so that adoption of analytics also requires substantial economic capital, a few tools are available for free, such as Google Analytics, albeit with limited capabilities compared with paid ones. Other news organizations have developed their own tools, such as *The Guardian, The New York Times*, and *The Financial Times*, patterned after web analytics products from the technological field but designed within journalism's internal logic. Some examples of web analytics tools include:

**Google Analytics**. This is a freemium web analytics service provided by Google. It was first introduced on 14 November 2005 after Google acquired the web analytics company, Urchin Software Corporation. It was launched for free and attracted a very high demand such that new sign-ups were stopped after one week (Clifton, 2015). Google Analytics collects a large amount of data, including but not limited to session duration (the time a visitor spends on a site), bounce rate (percentage of people that leave after viewing a single page), number of page views, and number of new users, among others. Generally, Google Analytics measures both user acquisition data and user behavior data. The former refers to intrinsic user data (e.g. age, gender) as well as acquisition data (where the visitors are coming from, such as via search engines or social media).

**Chartbeat**. This New York City-based company was launched in 2009 and claims to be working with more than 60,000 media brands across over 60 countries. It provides data on live visits, visitor frequency, visits by type device, sources of traffic, social media metrics, and a list of most viewed articles, and offers headline testing. Its website lists *The New York Times, The Washington Post, The Telegraph, The Atlantic, Le Monde*, and CNN as among its customers.

**Adobe Analytics**. In 2009, Adobe bought the web analytics tool Omniture and introduced Adobe Site Catalyst (Yang, 2012). Now called Adobe Analytics, this system tracks similar real-time metrics as other web analytics tool, such as page views, unique visitors, and views per type of device, among others. It is also used for observing trends over long periods, such as when news organizations compare website performance during the year's first quarter with the same period the previous year. Its website features "success stories" from electronics company Philips and airline company WestJet to measure customer interaction and experiences.

**SimilarWeb**. Founded in 2007 in Tel-Aviv, SimilarWeb provides a range of services that covers the areas of marketing, research, sales, and investors. For the publishing industry, prominent features are: (a) Website analysis, such as traffic sources, visits, and engagement rates; (b) traffic sources overview, which shows individual traffic channels and the traffic share per keyword, referring site, and social network; (c) audience interests, which shows the sites users visit before and after going to a particular site; (d) popular pages, which shows the most viewed pages and categories; and (e) outgoing ads, which analyzes sites to discover new advertisers. It also provides information about the performance of competitor sites. Its website lists *The Guardian*, Comcast, and National Geographic as some of its customers.

**Webtrekk**. Headquartered in Berlin since 2004, Webtrekk is a customer analytics platform that helps companies to analyze the behavior of their users on websites or mobile apps and compare data from the two platforms. It places a heavy emphasis on mobile applications, and offers app enhancement services such as sending user notifications about trending topics. Aside from providing analytics, it also offers audience segmentation and automated advertising. Its website lists several media companies in Germany as customers.

**Parse.ly**. Founded in 2009 in Philadelphia, Parse.ly started as a platform to deliver personalized content recommendations to users. But after publishers became interested in how Parse.ly predicted what would interest content users, the company introduced Parse.ly Dash in 2011 and provided services such as tracking metrics about topics, authors, sections, and referrers; identifying patterns and trends; and helping on marketing and promotion on social media (Kamdar, 2012). Dash later evolved into Parse.ly Analytics, which is the company's current analytics tool. It now updates real-time data while also providing historical reader trends. Its website lists *The Wall Street Journal*, Quartz, Slate, HuffPost, Bloomberg, and Conde Nast as among its customers.

**Ophan**. This is developed by the Guardian News & Media, which publishes *The Guardian* and *The Observer*. Launched in 2015, its purpose is to provide journalists with insights on their stories' performance (Shead, 2015). Similar to other analytics tools, such as Chartbeat, the in-house analytics engine has a dashboard format and tracks metrics such as page views, median attention time, what browser people are using, what countries visitors are from, among others. The insights help the digital team promote content and allow journalists to monitor traffic on their own stories and in making editorial judgments. A benefit of Ophan is that its design is meant to be intuitive, unlike other popular analytics tools that are thought to be too complex for normal journalists to use effectively. Its interface is thus designed to be similar to the Guardian's website (Shead, 2015).

**Stela**. An acronym for story and events analytics, Stela is *The New York Times*' custom-built, in-house analytics dashboard created in September 2015 (Wang, 2016). Similar to Ophan, Stela aims to gather data and present them in a way that's easy for journalists to use. Hence, its design and typefaces were designed to mimic the Times' brand. As of 2016, Stela had 1,300 monthly users across the entire Times news operation, including their London and Hong Kong bureaus (Wang, 2016). Stela is focused on analytics from individual article pages, such as page views and referrals. It gathers the data from the Times' desktop and mobile sites and all of their mobile apps. It tells what countries readers are from and how many are subscribers, registered users or anonymous. It also shows top comments and posts on Facebook and Twitter, and data is gathered in 10-minute increments. Like other analytics tools, Stela helps to guide editorial decisions: For example, journalists can use it to test and subsequently tweak their headlines (Wang, 2016).

**Lantern**. Launched on 17 March 2016, Lantern is an editorial analytics dashboard developed by *The Financial Times* (FT). It provides journalists with real-time data, with a focus on reader engagement instead of visits or page views. FT defines engagement as "depth of scroll, time spent on page, traffic source, and device breakdown" alongside "frequency of visits, time spent reading, and the volume of articles read" (The Financial Times, 2016). Journalists are given access to a general editorial dashboard as well as a "personalized, beat-specific analysis" that is curated by the audience engagement team. The goal is to enable the newsroom to be more attuned to reader preferences to help guide editorial decisions (The Financial Times, 2016).

Most of these products are considered *on-site* web analytics that measure traffic to the specific websites that they track, such as Chartbeat, as opposed to *off-site* web analytics that use various methods to offer audience data estimates across different websites, allowing website owners to track competitors (Clifton, 2009), such as Comscore, which collects survey data from audiences as well as data from a panel of users whose computers are equipped with monitoring software to provide audience data across media platforms (Beleaga & Geary, 2012). Comscore claims to have a panel of two million internet uses around the world, half of whom are in the US, who opt in to have their data collected and shared (Delo, 2011).

## Entering journalism

Audience measurement in journalism was originally intended for news organizations' business—and not editorial—operations (Petre, 2018). Normative roles of journalism have always been predicated on service to the public, which makes news audiences an important consideration, but it was always about providing audiences what they needed to know to make informed decisions, more than providing them with entertainment or humor (Weaver & Wilhoit, 1986). But as journalism became a lucrative business through a traditional advertising model, business logic has also permeated the journalistic field, with news organizations competing not only in the market for advertising, but also in the stock market, as many news organizations turned into media conglomerates and owners started diversifying their business interests to include non-journalistic ventures (McManus, 1992, 1994). This echoes Bourdieu's (2005) observation of the journalistic field as highly heterogeneous, which makes it vulnerable to the sway of economic pressures. The Worlds of Journalism Study, which involves a survey of journalists from 67 countries conducted between 2012 and 2016, found that journalists in many countries perceive that the influence of competition and profit-making pressures on their work has increased over the years.

Such business logic is what prompted many news organizations to adopt web analytics tools. When I visited a newsroom in the United States that had just purchased a web analytics service in May 2013, I was told that one of the reasons for the purchase was to help the newsroom to grow its online traffic. The installation of web analytics in the newsroom came with a specific instruction from the management for the newsroom to grow traffic by 10% from the previous year. Indeed, Chartbeat, a leading web analytics company that has focused on newsrooms, promises on its website that its services "help the world's leading media organizations understand, measure, and build business value from the attention earned by their written and video content" (Chartbeat, 2018).

An important context to the institutionalization of web analytics as part of journalistic routines is the capital instability that agents in the journalistic field are facing. Not only are audience numbers and, consequently, advertising revenues declining, but trust in the news media in many countries is also decreasing. Thus, both journalism's economic and cultural capital are on shaky grounds. This opens up the field to external influences (Tandoc, 2018). As newsrooms embrace web analytics with hopes that it will help them stabilize their audience numbers or, in the language of field theory, their economic capital, they are also inadvertently exposing their newsrooms to the influence of these new technologies.

Technology as a term did not figure prominently in Bourdieu's works with field theory, and for a good reason. Bourdieu considers technology as "socially shaped" (Sterne, 2003, p. 373), so technology does not exist as a separate entity that can be studied by itself, but one that is always tied to human practices. Therefore, web analytics as a form of technology is best understood as structured by human practices that, in turn, structures human practices (Sterne, 2003). So while web analytics shapes how journalists do their work, it is also important to understand how web analytics is also shaped by how technologists, business managers, and journalists negotiate its use.

Web analytics has become one way for managers and owners to get their journalists meet business expectations without feeling explicitly obligated to do so (Petre, 2018). For example, a study that involved observations and interviews with staff members at Chartbeat argued that the web analytics dashboard "is a technological artifact that extracts increased productivity from workers—but it does so in a way that obfuscates, rather than highlights, managerial influence in the newsroom" (Petre, 2018, p. 510). Thus, web analytics also serves as a conduit for business logic to permeate the journalistic field—at the same time, it also allows the entry of a technological logic into journalism.

In her observations at Chartbeat, *The New York Times*, and Gawker Media, Petre (2018) concluded that what made web analytics firms successful in getting newsrooms to adopt their tools was how they tried to align their products with journalistic values, in a way appearing to pay deference to journalists. Web analytics firms market their products to two distinct—although in smaller newsrooms they might be overlapping—groups: The buyer group, or those with the authority to allocate organizational resources to subscribing to analytics service, such as business managers; and the user group, or those who will be using the analytics platform on a daily basis, such as online editors (Petre, 2018). While the marketing efforts of analytics firms target the buyer group, as can be observed in how they highlight on their websites the impact of analytics on improving business performance, it is with the user group that the analytics firm communicates regularly once the technology is adopted, which means the user group can affect whether or not the newsroom keeps and renews its subscription

(Petre, 2018). For example, Chartbeat's staff members consistently assured journalists that Chartbeat's analytics only serve to support or corroborate what the journalists already know and designed the tool's dashboard in a way that deferred to the users' editorial judgment (Petre, 2018). While a competing product had included automated recommendations on article placements to boost traffic, bypassing human editorial judgment, Chartbeat did not include that function in their product (Petre, 2018).

In their interviews with managers of web analytics firms, Belair-Gagnon and Holton (2018, p. 502) also found that "by designing algorithms and toolkits tailored to individual news organizations' needs, [web analytics firms] have been able to make themselves a reflexive and routinized part of the news process," from planning coverage to repositioning content. In doing so, web analytics firms positioned themselves as routinizers, ensuring that web analytics becomes embedded in news routines by making their products easy to use as well as by coordinating with users regularly, making themselves part of the journalistic routine (Belair-Gagnon & Holton, 2018). Web analytics firms also positioned themselves as connectors, linking journalists not only with their audiences, but also with other stakeholders in the news company, such as the business department. This has the effect of unifying, to some extent, the news company's editorial and economic goals (Belair-Gagnon & Holton, 2018). By invoking routinizing and connective roles, web analytics firms de-emphasize among journalists their role as disruptors who are introducing new insights and practices in the newsroom (Belair-Gagnon & Holton, 2018). By playing by the rules of journalism, web analytics firms have negotiated their way into the journalistic field, quietly but surely, making their actual impact on journalism more challenging, but also more important, to decipher.

## References

Beasley, M. (2013). *Practical web analytics for user experience*. Waltham, MA: Morgan Kaufmann.

Belair-Gagnon, V., & Holton, A. E. (2018). Boundary work, interloper media, and analytics in newsrooms. *Digital Journalism, 6*(4), 492–508. doi:10.1080/21670811.2018.1445001

Beleaga, T., & Geary, J. (2012). ScorecardResearch (ComScore): What is it and what does it do? *The Guardian*, (April 23, 2012). Retrieved from https://www.theguardian.com/technology/2012/apr/23/scorecardresearch-tracking-trackers-cookies-web-monitoring

Benson, R. (1999). Field theory in comparative context: A new paradigm for media studies. *Theory and Society, 28*(3), 463–498.

Benson, R. (2004). Bringing the sociology of media back in. *Political Communication, 21*(3), 275–292. doi:10.1080/10584600490481299
Benson, R. (2006). News media as a "journalistic field": What Bourdieu adds to new institutionalism, and vice versa. *Political Communication, 23*(2), 187–202. doi:10.1080/10584600600629802
Benson, R., & Neveu, E. (2005). Introduction: Field theory as a work in progress. In R. Benson & E. Neveu (Eds.), *Bourdieu and the journalistic field* (pp. 1–28). Malden, MA: Polity Press.
Bourdieu, P. (1985). The social space and the genesis of groups. *Theory and Society, 14*(6), 723–744.
Bourdieu, P. (1986). The forms of capital. In J. Richardson (Ed.), *Handbook of theory and research for the sociology of education* (pp. 241–258). New York: Greenwood.
Bourdieu, P. (1998). *On television*. New York: The New Press.
Bourdieu, P. (2005). The political field, the social science field and the journalistic field. In R. Benson & E. Neveu (Eds.), *Bourdieu and the journalistic field* (pp. 29–47). Malden, MA: Polity Press.
Chartbeat. (2018). *About Chartbeat*. Retrieved from https://chart.bt/2B02Hdw
Cherubini, F., & Nielsen, R. K. (2016). *Editorial analytics: How news media are developing and using audience data and metrics*. Retrieved from https://bit.ly/2EMOPaD
Clifton, B. (2009). Improving the web with web analytics. *journalism.co.uk*. Retrieved from https://bit.ly/2PtrziS
Clifton, B. (2015). *Google analytics is 10 years old – What's changed?* Retrieved from https://bit.ly/1SzBkYu
Couldry, N. (2003). Media meta-capital: Extending the range of Bourdieu's field theory. *Theory and Society, 32*(5/6), 653–677. doi:10.2307/3649655
DAA. (2008). *Web analytics definitions*. Retrieved September 28, 2013, from Digital Analytics Association https://bit.ly/1nvRY1j
Delo, C. (2011). Your guide to who measures what in the online space. *Ad Age*. Retrieved from Ad Age website: https://bit.ly/2EabRHC
Emirbayer, M., & Johnson, V. (2008). Bourdieu and organizational analysis. *Theory and Society, 37*(1), 1–44. doi:10.1007/s11186-007-9052-y
The Financial Times. (2016). The Financial Times launches next-generation analytics tool for the newsroom. *The Financial Times*. Retrieved from https://on.ft.com/2QEXphu
Gans, H. J. (2003). *Democracy and the news*. New York: Oxford University Press.
Handley, R. L., & Rutigliano, L. (2012). Journalistic field wars: Defending and attacking the national narrative in a diversifying journalistic field. *Media, Culture & Society, 34*(6), 744–760. doi:10.1177/0163443712449500
Herman, E. S., & Chomsky, N. (2002). *Manufacturing consent: The political economy of the mass media*. New York: Knopf Doubleday Publishing Group.
Johnson, R. (1993). Editor's introduction: Pierre Bourdieu on art, literature and culture. In R. Johnson (Ed.), *The field of cultural production: Essays on art and literature* (pp. 1–28). New York: Columbia University Press.
Kamdar, S. (2012). *The history of Parse.ly's analytics dashboard*. Retrieved from https://bit.ly/2zInkuX

McChesney, R. W. (2013). *Digital disconnect: How capitalism is turning the internet against democracy*. New York: New Press.

McManus, J. (1992). Serving the public and serving the market: A conflict of interest? *Journal of Mass Media Ethics, 7*(4), 196–208. doi:10.1207/s15327728jmme0704_1

McManus, J. (1994). *Market-driven journalism: Let the citizen beware?* Thousand Oaks, CA: Sage Publications.

Neveu, E. (2007). Pierre Bourdieu. *Journalism Studies, 8*(2), 335–347. doi:10.1080/14616700601149026

Petre, C. (2018). Engineering consent. *Digital Journalism, 6*(4), 509–527. doi:10.1080/21670811.2018.1444998

Russell, A. (2007). Digital communication networks and the journalistic field: The 2005 French riots. *Critical Studies in Media Communication, 24*(4), 285–302. doi:10.1080/07393180701560880

Sallaz, J. J., & Zavisca, J. (2007). Bourdieu in American sociology, 1980–2004. *Annual Review of Sociology, 33*, 21–41. doi:10.2307/29737752

Shead, S. (2015). Guardian developers build journalist-friendly Google Analytics platform. *Techworld*. Retrieved from https://bit.ly/2UqROKu

Shoemaker, P. J., & Reese, S. D. (1996). *Mediating the message: Theories of influences on mass media content* (2nd ed.). White Plains, NY: Longman.

Shoemaker, P. J., & Vos, T. P. (2009). *Gatekeeping theory*. New York: Routledge.

Siapera, E., & Spyridou, L.-P. (2012). The field of online journalism: A Bourdieusian analysis. In E. Siapera & A. Veglis (Eds.), *The handbook of global online journalism* (pp. 77–98). Malden, MA: John Wiley & Sons, Inc.

Stempel, C. (2005). Adult participation sports as cultural capital: A test of Bourdieu's theory of the field of sports. *International Review for the Sociology of Sport, 40*(4), 411–432. doi:10.1177/1012690206066170

Sterne, J. (2003). Bourdieu, technique and technology. *Cultural Studies, 17*(3–4), 367–389. doi:10.1080/0950238032000083863a

Tandoc, E. (2018). Gatekeeping influences and journalistic capital: Proposing a mechanism of influence. *Journalism Studies, 19*(16), 2344–2358. doi:10.1080/1461670X.2017.1345320

Tandoc, E., & Jenkins, J. (2017). The Buzzfeedication of journalism? How traditional news organizations are talking about a new entrant to the journalistic field will surprise you! *Journalism, 18*(4), 482–500. doi:10.1177/1464884915620269

Wang, S. (2016). The New York Times is trying to narrow the distance between reporters and analytics data. *Nieman Journalism Lab*. Retrieved from https://bit.ly/2a2GlcO

Weaver, D. H., & Wilhoit, G. C. (1986). *The American journalist. A portrait of US news people and their work*. Bloomington: Indiana University Press.

Willig, I. (2013). Newsroom ethnography in a field perspective. *Journalism, 14*(3), 372–387. doi:10.1177/1464884912442638

Yang, N. (2012). How web analytics are shaping advertising dollars and the newsroom. *Editor & Publisher*. Retrieved from https://bit.ly/2RKz7jt

Zamith, R. (2018). Quantified audiences in news production. *Digital Journalism, 6*(4), 418–435. doi:10.1080/21670811.2018.1444999

# 4 Journalists adapting

Web analytics has been described to me by at least two top-level editors at an American newsroom as the "editorial crack." With numbers on the dashboard changing in real-time and headlines going up and down a list of most viewed articles, viewing web analytics can be exhilarating. "You can sit here," a managing editor told me from his desk, "and watch it, popping all night."

Using web analytics is like playing an online game, with the top scorers prominently displayed on the homepage. The managing editor starts his day by opening web analytics in his personal laptop at home, so he'd know the numbers even before leaving for work. It's like a gambling machine—you take a guess which story will get the most views, and then wait to see the numbers if you got it right.

Tools that allow the collection, storage, and analysis of big data have made analytics a norm across major industries (Columbus, 2017). When we conducted a survey way back in 2012 among members of the American Society of News Editors, our results showed that even at that time, 96.5% use web analytics in their newsrooms (see Tandoc & Jenner, 2016). While most of them—about 55%—pay for third-party analytics services, such as Chartbeat, some 41% use free web analytics tools, such as Google Analytics. Online newsrooms not using web analytics are now an exception rather than the rule.

Numerous studies have documented the use of web analytics in newsrooms across different media systems, such as in Australia (Hanusch, 2017), Austria (Schlemmer, 2016), Canada (Neheli, 2018), China (Wang, 2016), Greece (Giomelakis, Sidiropoulos, Gilou, & Veglis, 2018), Kenya (Bunce, 2017), the Netherlands (Welbers, van Atteveldt, Kleinnijenhuis, Ruigrok, & Schaper, 2016), Sweden (Karlsson & Clerwall, 2013), and the United Kingdom (Schlesinger & Doyle, 2015). These studies demonstrate how web analytics has become deeply embedded in online news routines around the world. But while web analytics provides journalists with a wealth of information about their audiences and what their audiences do with news content, it still does not provide a complete picture (Wiggins, 2007), leaving some room for editorial guesswork. How web analytics transforms—or not—how day-to-day journalism is conducted still depends on how journalists adopt and adapt analytics (Tandoc, 2014).

## Adopting and adapting

While many studies have explored how journalists use web analytics in their work and with what impact, only a few studies explored why journalists use web analytics to begin with. In this period when web analytics has become universal, such a question is easy to take for granted. But the reasons for adopting analytics are important in understanding how it is being used and how it is disrupting traditional journalism. For example, Boczkowski (2005) argued that technological adoption does not directly change journalistic routines. Instead, how a technology is understood in the newsroom and how it is integrated into its organizational culture largely determine the extent of its impact.

It became clear to me during my observations in newsrooms in the United States that for most big news organizations, the primary motivation for adopting web analytics is economic. Legacy news organizations seeing their audience numbers decrease pin their hopes on their online platforms to bring in audiences and revenues (Tandoc, 2014). Knowing what audiences want and what they do with news content is seen as an important strategy to increase audience numbers online. So while third-party web analytics services are not cheap, having web analytics still became a priority to survive. And while it is true that for most newsrooms, online news has not adequately offset the dwindling revenues from traditional news, growing audiences online as a form of cultural capital is still seen as important, so that when the time comes that a profitable business model online is found, such cultural capital can be converted into economic capital (Tandoc, 2015). This organizational mind-set is seen in how some news organizations set newsroom targets to grow audience numbers year by year. For many news organizations, using web analytics is about not being left behind.

For individual journalists, the reasons for using web analytics can vary. A survey of 360 American journalists conducted in 2015 found that journalists' personal attitudes toward the use of audience feedback, their perception of their knowledge and skill in using technology, as well as their organizational policy affected the extent to which they used web analytics in their news work (Tandoc & Ferrucci, 2017). As more and more employees are brought into the newsroom for their big data, rather than journalistic, backgrounds, and as online newsrooms become staffed by an increasingly younger staff, the use of web analytics becomes even more normalized. It's a technology that young journalists are now expected to know how to use. New editorial positions have also emerged, such as the "engagement editor" tasked to monitor audience metrics and make strategic recommendations based on these (Ferrer-Conill & Tandoc, 2018). The creation of these audience-related roles, elevated to the level of editors, legitimizes "the tasks involved in making sense of audience data as important journalistic functions" (Ferrer-Conill & Tandoc, 2018, p. 448). With the integration of these audience-related positions into the newsroom leadership, the role of audience metrics in editorial decisions also becomes institutionalized.

## Editorial guesswork

Web analytics is not a foolproof system. Web analytics data are based on "cookies" from websites that are deposited in a computer when a website is rendered by a web browser (Benkoil, 2010). But computer users can delete cookies before logging out or choose private browsing with some web browsers, so when these users log in on the same website again, they might be counted as a new user. On the other hand, when several people share the same computer, they might be counted as just one visitor. Online sites have considered user registration to address these issues with tracking visitors, but many users also get turned off by having to register (Bermejo, 2007).

Another issue is the selection of metrics to monitor and prioritize. What data should constitute key performance indicators? The industry of web analytics has shifted its standard from hits, to page views, to unique monthly visitors, to average time spent. However, each of these metrics has inherent weaknesses in terms of accurately capturing what it is that journalists hope to learn from web analytics (Krall, 2009).

A *hit* gets recorded when a requested page or an element on a page is downloaded to the user's browser. Hits are often inflated, because a single web page can contain multiple elements and therefore record multiple hits (Khoo et al., 2008). *Page views* refer to the number of times a page is viewed by a user, including multiple views of the same page by the same user (Khoo et al., 2008). A survey of 2,700 journalists and newsroom managers in 130 countries found that of the various available metrics from web analytics, newsrooms use *page views* the most (ICFJ, 2018). *Unique visitors* refers to the number of unique users visiting a site, measured based on anonymous cookies related to a user's browser, often aggregated based on a specific time span, usually on a per month basis. A user making multiple visits to the same site using the same computer within the month is counted as one unique visitor for that month. However, a user visiting the same website using two different computers within the month is counted as two unique visitors. Because of the limitations of these metrics, other publishers have pushed for considering *time spent* as the golden metric. Time spent refers to the amount of time a user spends on a page. For example, content-hosting site Medium measures "total reading time" to gauge reader engagement with its content (Davies, 2013). Still, the debate continues about which metrics accurately measure audience engagement and therefore should be prioritized (see Table 4.1).

While these gaps in web analytics are filled by other audience information systems, such as surveys and customer databases (Wiggins, 2007), they also leave wide spaces for editorial judgment. "Web analytics reveals what users do, but not why they do it" (Wiggins, 2007, p. 20).

*Table 4.1* Commonly tracked web metrics

| *Term* | *Definition* |
|---|---|
| Unique visitors | This refers to the total number of unique users that have visited the page or site at a specified period, usually for a month. |
| Page views | The number of times a page is loaded or reloaded in a browser. A single user can have multiple page views. |
| Time spent | This refers to the amount of time a visitor spends on a page or the site. |
| Bounce rate | This refers to the percentage of single-hit or single-page visits, or when a user opens a single page on the site and exits the site right after. |
| Return visits | This refers to the percentage of visits from returning users out of the total visits to the site. |
| Devices | Web analytics tools provide a breakdown of users based on the device they use to view the site: Desktop, tablet, or mobile. |
| Referrals | This refers to sources that refer traffic to the site, such as search engines and social media. |
| Social media | Web analytics tools also track social media engagement, such as number of Facebook shares or Twitter retweets. |

Note: Newsrooms track numerous metrics to have a better understanding of their audiences. This list includes only some of the most commonly tracked web metrics. Newsrooms monitor specific sets of metrics depending on their goals or strategies. For example, a newsroom that aims to meet goals of increasing traffic will likely focus on the number of unique visitors and return visits. Bounce rates will also be important, as examining a page with a high bounce rate might help reveal an issue that needs to be solved to help retain users to the site.

Shoemaker and Reese (2014) also argued that: "Audience research may give media workers ideas about the general interests of viewers, listeners, and readers, but it cannot help much in their daily choices" (p. 170). The need to fill these gaps in audience research rests on the shoulders of journalists, highlighting the tension between knowing what the audience wants and imposing one's news judgment and the prescriptions of the journalistic doxa.

## Using web analytics

A systematic way to understand how web analytics is used in day-to-day journalism is to examine how it figures in each of the different stages of news construction, from accessing information to selection and filtering, processing and editing, distribution, and interpretation (Domingo et al., 2008; Tandoc, 2014).

The *access and observation stage* refers to how journalists get to know or encounter newsworthy events or issues that can potentially be covered or reported about. Reporters are assigned to specific beats or topics, where they are expected to gather leads to potential stories. While the stereotypical image of a journalist is one who is busy responding to newsworthy events that unfold, most newsworthy events being reported are actually pre-scheduled (e.g. court hearings, press conferences, sporting events), and many news articles are pursued, discovered, or followed up on by journalists themselves (Boorstin, 1973; Gans, 1979). But in the age of web analytics, news editors also encounter newsworthy events or issues based on audience metrics, such as by looking at lists of trending topics on social media or lists of top-performing articles. In many newsrooms, editorial meetings conducted to plan the day's coverage start with a quick review of stories and topics that are trending, which are generated based on audience metrics (Tandoc, 2014; Welbers et al., 2016). Some newsrooms also track the analytics of their competitors to keep an eye on popular stories.

The *selection or filtering stage* refers to the point when journalists, after the initial encounter with events or issues, select which stories to pursue. In traditional journalism, this stage purely refers to selecting stories to report about. Since conducting interviews, writing articles or scripts, and editing require resources, selection is a crucial stage. Newspapers also have a limited number of pages and television news programs have a limited amount of airtime, so news coverage has to be carefully planned and selection has to be stringent. But in the age of digital journalism, such space limitations no longer exist. There is also an abundance of content, supplied by news wires as well as by non-journalists volunteering user-generated content. Thus, selection has increasingly shifted from selecting stories to pursue to selecting articles to publish. In the age of web analytics, story selection is increasingly influenced by audience numbers. Topics that are trending on social media get written about. Stories that are getting good numbers tend to be displayed more prominently and get follow-up stories.

Web analytics programs also make recommendations on which stories to select for which spot on the homepage, complete with an estimated number of additional traffic each recommendation can bring to the site (Tandoc, 2014). The process of *deselection* has also emerged. This is when editors need to decide which of the articles they have selected for publication on the homepage will be replaced by a more recent article or a better-performing one (Tandoc, 2014). *Deselection* is almost exclusively decided based on numbers. When the number of unique visitors to the site starts to dip, online editors take that as a cue to start moving things around on the homepage to stabilize site traffic. This includes deselecting a story that is no longer performing well based on numbers.

The *processing or editing* stage refers to reshaping news content. Traditionally, it refers to the stage when news articles are submitted by reporters to editors, who then edit the copy for both style and substance. For a newspaper, this is an important stage to make sure no typographical or factual errors end up on the printed copy. But in the age of digital journalism, a published article can be edited again. This has led to prioritizing speed over accuracy, especially on social media (Bruno, 2011). In the age of web analytics, published stories can be re-processed, especially if they are not performing well based on numbers. For example, some editors also update stories by adding a photo, an infographic, or a video to help the article perform better, especially after learning from experience with web analytics that adding visual complements to news stories can increase click-rates (Tandoc, 2014). Some analytics programs also provide a headline-testing service, where an editor can write two headlines for one story, then for a short time, the system randomly exposes readers to one of the two versions and then provides the editor a recommendation on which headline worked better in terms of getting users to read. Backed by audience data, the recommended headline always wins.

The *distribution stage* refers to how a news article gets disseminated to news audiences. While the traditional conceptualization of gatekeeping as a process culminates in news selection, with journalists selecting which articles to push out, publication no longer guarantees reaching an audience, especially in this period of information oversupply online. Web analytics influences news distribution in two ways. First, many news sites include lists of popular stories, automatically populated based on audience metrics, that serve as news recommendation tools for other users (Thorson, 2008). This practice, however, has slowed down, as online editors realized that keeping an automated list of most popular stories keeps the site stagnant—being in the list helps promote a story to other users, so the more likely it stays in the list, which then keeps the list almost the same throughout the day. A static list, however, is less likely to encourage repeat visits, since users will just find the same set of articles listed.

Second, news organizations have become very active in promoting their content on social media, as social media sites have become significant drivers of site traffic. While some newsrooms have set up a system where every article they upload on their site is automatically promoted on their Twitter accounts, such practice makes the tweets sounds impersonal, which is contrary to how social media works. Instead, many newsrooms seek to be strategic in pushing content out on social media, making sure they push out the right content at the right time on the right platform (Duffy, Ling, & Tandoc, 2017; Giomelakis et al., 2018; Hanusch, 2017). Selecting which articles to promote on social media is also often determined by audience metrics—popular stories tend to get promoted even further. A survey of 2,700 journalists and newsroom managers in 130 countries found that the most common use of web analytics is "to drive to their websites" (ICFJ, 2018, p. 50). This is often done by promoting articles that are already popular or are projected to be popular. Some newsrooms also allot resources to advertise some of their articles on Facebook, usually by paying for what Facebook terms as a "boost." Some editors consult web analytics to decide which articles to boost on Facebook.

The *interpretation stage* refers to making sense of the news. Domingo et al. (2008) operationalized user participation at this stage in terms of user comments to news articles, either within the news site or on other platforms, such as on reader forums or even social media. User comments also provide journalists with feedback about stories or about their news coverage. However, some journalists have negative perceptions of qualitative audience feedback (Anderson, 2011). Some publications have even closed down their comments section, citing how uncivil reader discourse can become. With user comments often ignored, journalists rely heavily on quantitative feedback from web analytics.

However, aside from figuring into the different stages of news construction, web analytics has also penetrated *newsroom management*. For example, some news organizations now use web analytics to measure the performance of their journalists. It has become common in many online newsrooms to introduce a reporter as someone who brings in the most page clicks. In his fieldwork at the Philadelphia Inquirer way back in 2008, Anderson (2011) came across a journalist carrying printed pages of a web analytics report that included a list of authors sorted based on click counts. The journalist said: "We're probably headed toward a new model where reporters get paid by clicks" (Anderson, 2011). That same year, Gawker Media launched a new system to award pay bonuses to writers based on the popularity of their posts (Boutin, 2008); it later experimented with a pay-per-click model and paid participants $5 per 1,000 unique monthly visitors (Fischer, 2014). A reporter working for an online-only news outlet in Hong Kong recalls a "comprehensive value system" from her previous workplace in China, where "if the page views of your story is high, you can get more points and that connects to the bonus."

Finally, web analytics also affects how news managers make sense of their audiences. Through web analytics, journalists get some clues to their readers' reading habits, such as how they encounter news articles (e.g. via social media or search engine), how they consume news (e.g. via mobile phones or using a desktop), and what time of the day they usually read news, among others. For example, an online editor in Singapore working for a television company's news site said they used to take it slow during weekends to let their journalists take some rest. "But when we saw that the reading patterns on the weekends seem to be slightly different from the weekdays—that mixed up our offerings. Then we decided to change our release times." This meant some adjustments when it comes to deployment of editors and reporters.

Web analytics also provides details of readers' geo-location. Such audience data has allowed news managers to segment audiences. For example, newsrooms can distinguish between loyal and local readers that consume stories on local politics, and one-time visitors that found the site through one viral story (Tandoc, 2014). While one-time visitors help increase audience size for the news site, they may not be the kind of audiences that local advertisers want. So for a small news site whose revenues come mainly from local advertisers, targeting local and loyal readers through localized content becomes the priority.

Such information about the audience also helps newsrooms to expand their target market. For example, a large news organization in Singapore discovered through web analytics that it was also getting a lot of clicks from China, but that readers in China navigate the site differently from readers in Singapore. Since Singapore is a relatively small market, it is a city-state of about five million people, being able to attract readers from China will be good for business. So, the news organization maintains different layouts for Singapore and China (Rahil, 2018). The website content is the same, but the design for readers in Singapore includes more visuals, while the design for readers in China focuses on text and includes a lot of hyperlinks (Rahil, 2018).

## Changes and continuities

Of course, usage patterns evolve over time. As web analytics becomes deeply embedded in news routines, the extent and ways it is used change as well. Newsroom ethnographies that documented web analytics use across different newsrooms, conducted at different time points, reveal how web analytics use has evolved (Anderson, 2011; Duffy et al., 2017; Ferrucci & Tandoc, 2015; Neheli, 2018; Nelson & Tandoc, 2018; Petre, 2018; Tandoc, 2014; Usher, 2013). For example, observations conducted at the same newsroom in the United States three years apart revealed continuities in usage patterns, such as in using analytics to test headlines and track page views (Nelson & Tandoc, 2018). "The immediate objective of growing traffic and the strategies to achieve it remain the same," the study observed (Nelson & Tandoc, 2018, p. 12). However, some journalists have become more reflective when it comes to realizing the dual goals they now have to pursue: Stories that do well based on traffic, and stories that are good for democracy (Nelson & Tandoc, 2018).

It will also be helpful to compare specific usage patterns over time. In the course of my research on web analytics in journalism, I have also tracked usage patterns through surveys of journalists. I have done two of such surveys in the United States. The first one was conducted in 2013 for my dissertation and involved 206 online editors (Tandoc, 2015). The second one was conducted in 2015 for a collaborated project and involved 360 online journalists (Tandoc & Ferrucci, 2017). It is crucial to note that these two samples are different—the first one focused only on online editors and excluded reporters, while the second one did not distinguish between editors and reporters, as long as they worked for an online newsroom. Still, a quick comparison of the results offers some idea on how specific usage patterns might be evolving (see Table 4.2).

Both surveys asked respondents to indicate how often they used web analytics data for each of at least 16 different uses, a scale I developed based on my interviews with journalists and observations at three online newsrooms (Tandoc, 2014). Overall, in both 2013 and 2015, the use

*Table 4.2* Using web analytics

| *Specific use* | *2013* | *2015* |
|---|---|---|
| To determine which stories are doing well | 79.3 | 77.2 |
| To monitor how the story I wrote/edited is doing | 53.5 | 69.7 |
| To determine where traffic is coming from | 63 | 64.3 |
| To determine which stories are not doing well | 64.3 | 59 |
| To know which topic areas to increase coverage in | 30.9 | 49.7 |
| To determine what stories to do follow ups on | 35.6 | 44.6 |
| To determine story placement in the homepage | 42.6 | 43.9 |
| To monitor if the site is working properly | 42.5 | 43.6 |
| To improve user experience | 42.3 | 41.8 |
| To decide how to write the headline | 29.2 | 35.7 |
| To decide which stories to cover | 14.6 | 35.5 |
| To help design the website | 27.9 | 23.1 |
| To determine how to cover a story | 13.5 | 22 |
| To plan deployment of reporters | 14.9 | 19.5 |
| To help evaluate the performance of employees | 9.7 | 18.8 |
| To know where to increase coverage in terms of geographic location | 11.5 | 18.8 |

Note: The figures represent percentage of respondents who reported using web analytics for each specific use "often" or "very often." The 2015 survey involved 360 online journalists in the United States, while the 2013 survey involved 206 online editors in the United States.

of web analytics to track audience size was the most common. Tracking which stories are doing well, monitoring the performance of an article one has written or edited, and determining where traffic comes from were among the highest ranked uses. These uses are some of what I had considered as *traffic-oriented use*, or using data from web analytics to monitor traffic (Tandoc, 2015).

What is interesting is the increase in the frequency of using web analytics to determine topic areas to pursue and specific stories to follow up. In the 2013 survey, 30.9% of the respondents said they used web analytics often or very often to determine which topic areas to increase coverage in, while in the 2015 survey, 49.7% reported engaging in such use often or very often (see Table 4.2). Similarly, using web analytics often or very often to determine which stories to cover increased from only 14.6% in 2013 to 35.5% in 2015. These uses are what I referred to as *content-oriented use*, or using web analytics to make editorial decisions, such as planning coverage and allocating newsroom resources (Tandoc, 2015). There also seems to be a marked increase in the extent to which web analytics is used for newsroom management. In both surveys, I asked respondents how often they use web analytics to "help evaluate the performance of employees." In 2013, only 9.7% responded often or very often—this increased to 18.8% when I asked the question again in 2015.

Earlier studies on how journalists used web analytics documented usage patterns at the very last stages of gatekeeping (Anderson, 2011; Lee, Lewis, & Powers, 2014; Vu, 2013). Monitoring traffic, rewriting headlines, and determining story placement on the website are editorial decisions made after stories have been planned, selected, and written. However, recent studies have also focused on the increasing use of analytics to determine topics to pursue or plan the deployment of resources (Welbers et al., 2016; Wendelin, Engelmann, & Neubarth, 2015), decisions that are made at the earlier stages of gatekeeping (Tandoc & Jenner, 2016). As expected, the ways in which web analytics is used in the newsroom are evolving. But it also means that its impact on news work is also changing.

## Shaping usage patterns

While many online newsrooms use web analytics, how they use it and how they make sense of audience metrics vary. While web analytics plays a major role in some newsrooms, it exerts a weak influence in editorial decisions in others. Individual journalists also use web analytics in different ways and degrees. For example, interviews with 67 foreign correspondents in East and West Africa identified three types of journalists when it comes to web analytics use: The first group refers to *data-driven* correspondents, or those who use web analytics data routinely in their work (Bunce, 2015). The second group, which accounts for the majority of those interviewed, refers to *data-informed* journalists who have only a little knowledge about audience data from their organizations, but are sometimes guided by their editors, who routinely access analytics, in pursuing popular topics (Bunce, 2015). Finally, a small minority can be considered *data denialists* or those "oblivious to readership data" and who are not informed about audience data nor feel guided by audience metrics in their work (Bunce, 2015, p. 23).

Studies have documented different factors that affect the extent to which web analytics is used in the newsroom. Some have focused on the role of *individual journalists*. For example, while those in managerial positions (e.g. chief editor, managing editor) focus on tracking long-term metrics, such as monitoring unique visitors per month, online editors focus on real-time metrics, such as page views per article, that are useful for day-to-day operations (Tandoc, 2014). In terms of frequency of use, a survey of 358 journalists in Australia found that while 33.2% use web analytics at least once a day, with about 10% reporting they use analytics several times per hour, mid-level officers, such as news directors and section editors, use web analytics more often than did reporters or newsroom managers (Hanusch & Tandoc, 2017).

Other studies also noted differences between *news organizations* when it comes to web analytics use. For example, Karlsson and Clerwall (2013, p. 74) found that while commercial outlets tend to monitor analytics in real time, public service media outlets use web analytics "more as an after-the-fact evaluation rather than as a real-time assessment." The availability and accessibility of web analytics tools also influenced the extent to which they are used. For example, web analytics is used more frequently in news organizations that display the metrics openly, such as through large monitors erected in the middle of the newsroom, than in newsrooms that provide limited access to analytics, such as through occasional emails to journalists (Welbers et al., 2016).

Online newsrooms affiliated with a traditional platform with a longer history also find themselves having to align their news judgment with that of their traditional legacy platforms. For example, a social media editor in Singapore said: "At the end of the day, your online [and offline] product cannot be too divorced from each other, they must have a common identity, so it cannot be your online site is so salacious and your print so proper; the standard must be equal" (Rahil, 2018).

While many studies have examined the use of web analytics in digital-native and traditional newsrooms, less attention has been paid to examining how news wire agencies use web analytics. What is different is that for wire agencies, such as the Associated Press and Reuters, their main audiences are other news outlets subscribing to their feeds. However, many wire agencies have also started their own websites where readers can directly access some of their articles, allowing them to track audience data. Some wire agencies, such as the Australian Associated Press, use analytics tools to monitor how their content is used by news outlets that subscribe to their service (Schlemmer, 2017). However, access to this tool is only for editors. "I don't want to give the journalists the wrong idea," said Tony Gillies, AAP's editor-in-chief. "I don't want journalists thinking of how to change their work. I don't want them under added pressure, worried they have not written as many stories as the person next to them" (Schlemmer, 2017).

A news organization's market orientation also matters. A comparison of two newsrooms in the United States found that "the strongly market-oriented newsroom used analytics extensively while the weakly market-oriented newsroom used analytics less frequently, with only a few editors accessing their analytics usually once a week" (Ferrucci & Tandoc, 2015, p. 70). Interviews with American journalists from news organizations with different levels of market orientation also found that while in weakly market-oriented newsrooms, web analytics data is mostly used to reorganize the website, in strongly market-oriented newsrooms, "more editorial decisions about what to cover were made based on these data" (Ferrucci, 2018, p. 14). While journalists at Al Jazeera recognized how important web analytics are, they often also disregarded audience metrics when it came to making editorial decisions (Usher, 2013). Since Al Jazeera is funded by its government, the pressure to increase web traffic is almost non-existent, compared with commercial newsrooms.

A less explored, but nonetheless important, factor in understanding how web analytics is used in newsrooms is the *social context* where the newsroom and its journalists operate. For example, interviews with journalists in Singapore, a small but economically advanced nation also known for its closely regulated media system, found that while journalists in the country are aware of how web analytics is used in newsrooms in Western countries, they use web analytics more carefully (Rahil, 2018). For example, chasing clicks must be balanced with the need to treat sensitive topics, such as politics, race, and religion, more cautiously. If these are at odds, journalists prioritize caution over clicks (Rahil, 2018).

## Editorial crack

Describing web analytics as the "editorial crack" is both funny and provocative (Tandoc, 2014). It is a good metaphor, capturing how using web analytics can be addictive, that some journalists even access their news organization's web analytics dashboard on their mobile phones (Petre, 2018). But where does the metaphor stop, for while crack, the slang for cocaine, is addictive, it is also dangerous and can impair thinking?

Crack, as a noun, also refers to a gap or narrow space created when something breaks. In a period when traditional journalism seems to be breaking—traditional revenue sources are drying up; non-journalists are performing journalistic acts; fake news competes for audience attention—web analytics can be the crack that allows external forces to penetrate the journalistic field. But does this fill the gap or widen it instead?

Some sound the alarm on the potential negative impact on journalism of how web analytics is being used, making journalists more reliant on audience preferences in their day-to-day decision-making (Anderson, 2011; Tandoc & Thomas, 2014), but some question whether web analytics exerts any significant effects on news construction to begin with (Zamith, 2018).

Web analytics has become embedded in work routines in many newsrooms around the world, reaching the state of "taken-for-grantedness" (Ling, 2012). This is when web analytics finally becomes invisible in the newsroom, and when its impact becomes all the more significant.

## References


Anderson, C. W. (2011). Between creative and quantified audiences: Web metrics and changing patterns of newswork in local US newsrooms. *Journalism, 12*(5), 550–566. doi:10.1177/1464884911402451

Benkoil, D. (2010). What web analytics can – and can't – tell you about your site's traffic and audience. *Poynter*. Retrieved from https://bit.ly/2VUSngm

Bermejo, F. (2007). *The internet audience: Constitution and measurement*. New York: Peter Lang Publishing Inc.

Boczkowski, P. J. (2005). *Digitizing the news: Innovation in online newspapers*. Cambridge, MA: MIT Press.

Boorstin, D. (1973). *The image: A guide to pseudo-event in America*. New York: Atheneum.

Boutin, P. (2008). Denton to pay bloggers based on traffic. *Gawker*. Retrieved from https://bit.ly/2SK68MR

Bruno, N. (2011). Tweet first, verify later? How real-time information is changing the coverage of worldwide crisis events. *Reuters Institute for the Study of Journalism*. Retrieved from https://bit.ly/2Fuiztg

Bunce, M. (2015). Africa in the click stream: Audience metrics and foreign correspondents in Africa. *African Journalism Studies, 36*(4), 12–29. doi:10.1080/23743670.2015.1119487

Bunce, M. (2017). Management and resistance in the digital newsroom. *Journalism*. doi:10.1177/1464884916688963

Columbus, L. (2017). 53% of companies are adopting big data analytics. *Forbes*. Retrieved from https://bit.ly/2UTaJOe

Davies, P. (2013). *Medium's metric that matters: Total time reading*. Retrieved from https://bit.ly/UtjmyT

Domingo, D., Quandt, T., Heinonen, A., Paulussen, S., Singer, J. B., & Vujnovic, M. (2008). Participatory journalism practices in the media and beyond. *Journalism Practice, 2*(3), 326–342. doi:10.1080/17512780802281065

Duffy, A., Ling, R., & Tandoc, E. C. (2017). The people have spoken (the bastards?): Finding a legitimate place for feedback in the journalistic field. *Journalism Practice*, 1–18. doi:10.1080/17512786.2017.1372696

Ferrer-Conill, R., & Tandoc, E. (2018). The audience-oriented editor: Making sense of the audience in the newsroom. *Digital Journalism, 6*(4), 436–453. doi: 10.1080/21670811.2018.1440972

Ferrucci, P. (2018). It is in the numbers: How market orientation impacts journalists' use of news metrics. *Journalism*. doi:10.1177/1464884918807056

Ferrucci, P., & Tandoc, E. (2015). A tale of two newsrooms: How market orientation affects web analytics use. In W. Gibbs & J. McKendtrick (Eds.),

*Contemporary research methods and data analytics in the news industry* (pp. 58–76). Philadelphia: IGI Global.

Fischer, M. C. (2014). The pay-per-visit debate: Is chasing viral traffic hurting journalism? *American Journalism Review*. Retrieved from https://bit.ly/1i1pAvx

Gans, H. (1979). *Deciding what's news* (1st ed.). New York: Pantheon Books.

Giomelakis, D., Sidiropoulos, E., Gilou, S., & Veglis, A. (2018). The utilization of web analytics in online Greek journalism. *Journalism Studies*, 1–22. doi:10.1080/1461670X.2017.1412805

Hanusch, F. (2017). Web analytics and the functional differentiation of journalism cultures: Individual, organizational and platform-specific influences on newswork. *Information, Communication & Society, 20*(10), 1571–1586. doi: 10.1080/1369118X.2016.1241294

Hanusch, F., & Tandoc, E. (2017). Comments, analytics, and social media: The impact of audience feedback on journalists' market orientation. *Journalism*. doi:10.1177/1464884917720305

ICFJ. (2018). *The state of technology in global newsrooms*. Retrieved from https://bit.ly/2TTsvzT

Karlsson, M., & Clerwall, C. (2013). Negotiating professional news judgment and "clicks": Comparing tabloid, broadsheet and public service traditions in Sweden. *Nordicom Review, 34*(2), 65. doi:10.2478/nor-2013-0054

Khoo, M., Pagano, J., Washington, A. L., Recker, M., Palmer, B., & Donahue, R. A. (2008). *Using web metrics to analyze digital libraries*. Paper presented at the Proceedings of the 8th ACM/IEEE-CS Joint Conference on Digital Libraries, Pittsburgh, PA.

Krall, J. (2009). Using social metrics to evaluate the impact of online healthcare communications. *Journal of Communication in Healthcare, 2*(4), 387–394. doi:10.1179/cih.2009.2.4.387

Lee, A. M., Lewis, S. C., & Powers, M. (2014). Audience clicks and news placement: A study of time-lagged influence in online journalism. *Communication Research, 41*(4), 505–530. doi:10.1177/0093650212467031

Ling, R. (2012). *Taken for grantedness: The embedding of mobile communication into society*. Cambridge, MA: The MIT Press.

Neheli, N. B. (2018). News by numbers. *Digital Journalism, 6*(8), 1041–1051. doi: 10.1080/21670811.2018.1504626

Nelson, J. L., & Tandoc, E. (2018). Doing "well" or doing "good": What audience analytics reveal about journalism's competing goals. *Journalism Studies*, 1–17. doi:10.1080/1461670X.2018.1547122

Petre, C. (2018). Engineering consent. *Digital Journalism, 6*(4), 509–527. doi:10.1080/21670811.2018.1444998

Rahil, S. (2018). *Memes & the comedy of errors: How audience analytics is changing the news media in Singapore*. Paper presented at the International Communication Association Preconference on Audience Analytics, Prague.

Schlemmer, C. (2016). Speed is not everything: How news agencies use audience metrics. *Reuters Institute Fellowship Paper*. Retrieved from https://bit.ly/2rHP4LS

Schlemmer, C. (2017). How news agencies are using audience metrics, overcoming challenges. *Mediashift*. Retrieved from https://bit.ly/2CseJNq

Schlesinger, P., & Doyle, G. (2015). From organizational crisis to multiplatform salvation? Creative destruction and the recomposition of news media. *Journalism, 16*(3), 305–323. doi:10.1177/1464884914530223

Shoemaker, P. J., & Reese, S. D. (2013). *Mediating the message in the 21st century: A media sociology perspective* (3rd ed.). New York: Routledge.

Tandoc, E. (2014). Journalism is twerking? How web analytics is changing the process of gatekeeping. *New Media & Society, 16*(4), 559–575. doi:10.1177/1461444814530541

Tandoc, E. (2015). Why web analytics click: Factors affecting the ways journalists use audience metrics. *Journalism Studies, 16*(6), 782–799. doi:10.1080/1461670X.2014.946309

Tandoc, E., & Ferrucci, P. (2017). Giving in or giving up: What makes journalists use audience feedback in their news work? *Computers in Human Behavior, 68*, 149–156. doi:10.1016/j.chb.2016.11.027

Tandoc, E., & Jenner, M. (2016). Analyzing web analytics: How newsrooms use web metrics in news construction and why. *Journal of Applied Journalism & Media Studies, 5*(3), 423–440. doi:10.1386/ajms.5.3.423_1

Tandoc, E., & Thomas, R. (2014). The ethics of web analytics: Implications of using audience metrics in news construction. *Digital Journalism, 3*(2), 243–258. doi:10.1080/21670811.2014.909122

Thorson, E. (2008). Changing patterns of news consumption and participation. *Information, Communication and Society, 11*(4), 473–489. doi:10.1080/13691180801999027

Usher, N. (2013). Al Jazeera English online: Understanding web metrics and news production when a quantified audience is not a commodified audience. *Digital Journalism, 1*(3), 335–351. doi:10.1080/21670811.2013.801690

Vu, H. T. (2013). The online audience as gatekeeper: The influence of reader metrics on news editorial selection. *Journalism, 15*(8), 1094–1110. doi:10.1177/1464884913504259

Wang, Q. (2016). Participatory journalism in the Chinese context: Understanding journalism as process in China's participatory culture. *Journalism, 18*(4), 501–517. doi:10.1177/1464884916636177

Welbers, K., van Atteveldt, W., Kleinnijenhuis, J., Ruigrok, N., & Schaper, J. (2016). News selection criteria in the digital age: Professional norms versus online audience metrics. *Journalism, 17*(8), 1037–1053. doi:10.1177/1464884915595474

Wendelin, M., Engelmann, I., & Neubarth, J. (2015). User rankings and journalistic news selection. *Journalism Studies*, 1–19. doi:10.1080/1461670X.2015.1040892

Wiggins, A. (2007). Data-driven design: Using web analytics to validate heuristics. *Bulletin of the American Society for Information Science and Technology (Online), 33*(5), 20–24.

Zamith, R. (2018). Quantified audiences in news production. *Digital Journalism, 6*(4), 418–435. doi:10.1080/21670811.2018.1444999

# 5 Changing journalism

One of the things that drew me to practicing journalism was the impression that journalistic work is a daily adventure, with each day supposedly unpredictable. When I started working as a newspaper reporter in 2003, I soon realized that this impression was not entirely accurate. Journalistic work is also routinized. Of course, some days were still unpredictable, and the occasional, random threats I got from anonymous callers unhappy with my articles made my journalism stint interesting. I covered the crime beat for almost three years, and most days were marked by me going around police headquarters, local courts, and city hall offices in the morning; interviewing sources; submitting my news summaries by 1:30pm; and then submitting the stories I had written by 5pm. I would get a few phone calls from editors working on my stories later in the afternoon. If there were no other breaking stories, I would head back for dinner and call it a day.

When I was assigned to political beats, I had to deal with different types of news sources, but the stages were almost the same. Instead of going around police stations or rushing to crime scenes, I had to attend committee hearings and press conferences. Still, news summaries had to be in by 1:30pm; full articles had to be submitted by 5pm; editors would phone me to verify a few things; and then I'd call it a day.

Things soon changed.

Our news organization, which was also operating a news website aside from the newspaper where I was working, joined the convergence bandwagon and started requiring newspaper reporters to also break stories to the website. That meant phoning or emailing several paragraphs as soon as a press conference, or a court hearing, or an interview had ended, instead of waiting for the 5pm deadline that I had become used to. Newspaper reporters were initially paid extra for breaking news stories; soon, it became a regular part of our daily work. When social media became big, reporters were also asked to submit tweets while covering events. This meant alternating between writing down notes, interviewing sources, transcribing those interviews, writing a breaking news story, and writing the longer article for the newspaper, while sending updates for social media throughout the day.

In an increasing number of newsrooms, reporters are also now encouraged, if not expected, to promote their own work by sharing links, actively taking part in news distribution, when in the past reporters did not really have to bother much with how their work was disseminated. Now, some reporters even receive regular web analytics reports, helping them keep track of the reach of their own stories online and on social media.

While new technologies have simplified some processes, new ways of doing have also given journalists more things to do. And while the number of tasks related to news production and distribution has increased, the number of full-time journalists in many countries continues to dwindle, some reflecting layoffs and company closures (Armentrout, 2018; Channick, 2013; Edmonds, 2013; Seow, 2017; Spence, 2015). "The landscape changed very quickly. Lots of journalists lost their jobs," an editor-in-chief of a newsroom in the United States, who has moved across several newsrooms in the last 20 years or so, told me in 2013. "It meant smaller newsrooms had to do more with less. Editors had to do more with less. And it was kind of, you know, either change or die."

## Analytics as change

The introduction of new technology almost always leads to changes, and it is usually not a matter of if, but rather of how and to what extent. Pavlik (2000) argued that technological change affects how journalists do their jobs, the nature of news content they produce, news organizations and the industry as a whole, and the relationships between journalists and external actors. While many studies argue that technology "may not be the main driving force of developments in online journalism" (Steensen, 2011, p. 321), technology has always played an influential role (Pavlik, 2000).

Web analytics is a technological innovation. While it was developed not specifically for journalism, web analytics companies now specifically target news companies in marketing their services (Petre, 2018). Web analytics is now embedded in journalistic routines, but its impact on news production is neither direct nor automatic (Tandoc, 2015). Indeed, studies have argued that journalists usually normalize new technologies, using new tools in ways that fit their existing routines, instead of transforming their routines around new affordances (Lasorsa, Lewis, & Holton, 2011; Singer, 2005). For example, even with Twitter's retweeting, replying, and linking affordances, many journalists rarely used these features "either to open the gates to non-professional participants in the news production process or to offer information that could contribute to their accountability or transparency" (Lasorsa et al., 2011, p. 31).

A number of factors account for this. For example, journalists' years of socialization into traditional ways of doing cannot easily be undone. Some journalists, such as those working for big news companies with stable financial resources, might also have less motivation and incentive to change how they do things (Lasorsa et al., 2011). Journalists' skill sets and attitudes toward new technologies also affect the extent to which such technologies are adopted (Spyridou, Matsiola, Veglis, Kalliris, & Dimoulas, 2013). Some studies argued that because of these, "the potential of technology is severely mitigated" (Spyridou et al., 2013, p. 92). This sentiment also echoes in the journalism industry. For example, the social media director of one newsroom I visited in the United States said, referring to the journalistic field: "We were unwilling to accept evolution in the industry and that is what got us off track in the first place."

However, arguments such as these assume, to a large extent, that fully embracing technology is inherently positive and ought to be done. Others argued that traditional norms and routines persist for a good reason, and that technology can exert both positive and negative impacts (Tandoc & Thomas, 2014; Thomas, 2016). But how does web analytics, as a technological innovation, impact journalists, the content they produce, the culture of their news organizations, and their relationships with their publics?

## Impact on journalists

The constant supply of different forms of audience feedback into the newsroom has created additional tasks for journalists. Web analytics supplies real-time information about the audience, so someone has to make sense of that information. In the past, monitoring audience sizes was a task undertaken by a newsroom's marketing department. Now, in bigger newsrooms, the institutionalization of web analytics has given rise to new editorial positions, such as having an audience engagement editor, so audience tracking is completed right within editorial spaces (Ferrer-Conill & Tandoc, 2018). In smaller newsrooms, however, online editors are expected to keep an eye on audience metrics and make decisions based on these pieces of information. This is on top of their regular duties of editing, uploading, and promoting stories.

Having such a workload for online journalists has implications. First, it can lower job satisfaction and result in burnout. When I did observations at a big newsroom in the United States, my contact person was a digital editor who was just in her sixth month with the news company. I saw her edit stories, promote content on Twitter, help other editors with their social media accounts, and monitor the newsroom's analytics. Most of the time, she left the office way past the actual end of her work shift. When I completed my manuscript and sent her summaries of my findings about six months later, she had already left the newsroom and found a new job with a civic organization.

Seeing the metrics for their stories can also be a source of pride or confusion, and receiving hints or in some cases explicit instructions to go after popular topics can also be a source of frustration. "Some of my bosses, they are just interested in page views, they aren't interested in the news value, about the reporter's effort," a desk editor working for an online-only news outlet in Hong Kong said. "And I am very frustrated about it."

Second, having too many things to do also means having less time for reflections. I have observed how online editors behave during peak hours as well as during slow days. Slow days are marked by a lot of discussion between editors about some editorial decisions they have made. For example, during one slow and stormy afternoon at one of the newsrooms I undertook observations at in the United States, I heard the two online editors discuss the range of stories they had uploaded on the homepage. "I feel bad that we have Amanda [Bynes] and Beyonce both in the latest news," one of the editors said, just past 1pm. They agreed to move the Amanda Bynes story down.

How did that even happen that a news website known for its local news coverage would have two celebrity articles in its latest news section? Because of the winter storm, the newsroom had to deal with a lot of weather stories earlier in the day. Based on web analytics, the online editors know that online readership peaks between 11am and 1pm—during lunchtime, office workers go on a break and browse the web in between. Weather stories also tend to get a lot of page views. So, peak hours are when online editors switch from editing to uploading to promoting stories. It is also when they do not usually have adequate time to deeply reflect on every single editorial decision they make.

The use of web analytics for management purposes, such as to reward journalists whose articles do well in terms of audience metrics, also has implications for how individual journalists make sense of their own work. Not only do some journalists check their own news judgment with audience metrics (Arenberg & Lowrey, 2018), but some have questioned their roles in a newsroom that prioritizes numbers (Neheli, 2018). A journalist at a local newsroom in Canada lamented: "We're paying journalists a lot of money to be technicians" (Neheli, 2018, p. 1046). The fact that some journalists get rewarded for the clicks their articles bring has also caused some discord in the newsroom (Neheli, 2018). For some journalists, however, producing stories that do well in terms of audience metrics has become a badge of honor. In one of the biggest news outlets in Singapore, a multi-media journalist said that he and his peers have been including web analytics data in their annual appraisal submissions: "When we justify to our bosses why we deserve a promotion, now people are including the [number of] shares in their submissions."

Thus, web analytics also affects how journalists view their roles. The study of journalistic roles is important as it can affect how journalists do their work and, subsequently, the work that gets produced (Hanitzsch & Vos, 2016; Mellado, 2015). While the initial assumption, that how journalists view their roles affect their news outputs, has been questioned, especially since news outputs are usually organizational products (Mellado & Van Dalen, 2013; Tandoc, Hellmueller, & Vos, 2013), journalistic role conceptions can shape other types of journalistic decisions, such as what journalists say on their social media accounts, which can also reach a sizable audience (Tandoc, Cabañes, & Cayabyab, 2018).

In a survey of 358 news journalists in Australia, we found that how effective journalists perceive web analytics to be in helping them to understand the audience was positively related to their perception that consumer orientation has become more important over the years (Hanusch & Tandoc, 2017). Consumer orientation, as opposed to civic orientation, refers to focusing on providing content that appeals to more audiences. In other words, it seems that the presence of web analytics in newsrooms makes journalists perceive consumer-oriented roles to have become more salient than in the past. This is plausibly because "the nature of the feedback supplied by web analytics lends itself well to the purposes of the market, as audience behavior and preferences are presented in quantified forms" (Hanusch & Tandoc, 2017, p. 14). It is possible that routine exposure to audience preferences might lead to journalists believing that serving those preferences is an important editorial goal.

## News content

The accessibility and omnipresence of audience metrics in newsrooms that use them have also affected the range and format of news content that newsrooms produce. For example, a digital editor working for the website of a newspaper in Hong Kong said his news organization now covers some topics that it did not really pay much attention before. Asked to give an example, he replied: "Kitty news."

Cat posts have become emblematic of how journalism has changed (Ehrlich, 2014). The news and entertainment site BuzzFeed rose to internet stardom through its viral quizzes, lists, and—among a few other things—cat videos (Tandoc & Jenkins, 2017). The quantification of audience behavior partly made this possible—web analytics enabled newsrooms to see which posts got the most clicks. So many newsrooms now know for certain that weather is another hot topic among audiences. "It's very technical news and boring news," the digital editor in Hong Kong said. "But now, as we found [using analytics], people are actually interested in this kind of news. So we wrote more of this kind of news."

In the past, when most journalists relied on their own news judgment and their assumptions of what their audiences want, they had more control over news selection. But seeing the preferences of their actual audiences has made journalists select news stories that they would otherwise discard. "Sometimes, it makes me have to do some stories that are very strange," a journalist writing for a newspaper website in Singapore said. "Sometimes, maybe the top story is a very bizarre thing, and then because it's trending, I will find a way to legitimize it." A desk editor working at an online-only news outlet in Hong Kong said web analytics has also affected how journalists select news sources to interview. Some news sources, he pointed out, are very popular on social media and quoting them in an article can help the article go viral.

During my observations at newsrooms in the United States, a managing editor at a large newsroom in the Midwest told me that his news judgment would sometimes clash with the preferences of his audience as communicated through web analytics. Thus, his editorial decisions have become a series of balancing acts. "You know, we need to give them the spinach news—what's going on with the welfare reform—but we also need to make sure that we give them something they'll actually click on." Offering audiences some spinach also includes encouraging them to consume it. So how do you make readers click on a story on welfare reform? The metro editor at the same newsroom said journalists have to make an important but boring issue more interesting "So the spinach," the editor said, "you dress it up with a little lemon or a little garlic, you know?" A human interest angle, a photo gallery, or an infographic accompanying the story might do the trick.

Sometimes, online editors just have to compromise. "I know when I'm working on the web, there will be clickbaits and that sometimes feels like cotton candy," a web editor in the United States said. "But sometimes you have to hold your nose." Holding your nose is in keeping with the reality that news sites need to generate traffic.

The use of web analytics also has implications for local coverage. For example, observations at a local newsroom in Canada showed that some journalists worry that too much focus on audience metrics might compromise coverage of local stories (Neheli, 2018). The local newsroom produces both a print and an online version, and while the print version has a strong focus on local issues, the website often publishes international stories that have gone viral in order to attract traffic (Neheli, 2018). A study that compared two community news organizations also found that "the organization that more strongly emphasizes metrics publishes fewer in-depth civic issue stories" (Arenberg & Lowrey, 2018, p. 1), pointing to a potential link between the extent of web analytics use in a newsroom and the kind of content that the newsroom subsequently produces.

## Organizational culture

The organization plays a crucial role in the adoption and adaption of web analytics in the newsroom. Not only does the news organization decide whether or not to pay for and subscribe to web analytics or create their own proprietary analytics platform (Westlund & Ekstrom, 2018), but it also often outlines how web analytics should be used and for what purposes, shaping how the technology then affects newsroom cultures. For example, a digital editor for a newspaper website in Hong Kong said:

> Because the management started to weigh the analytics, the page views, as a more important index for performance of departments, there are so many topics that they will never touch before because they think that they are not news, but now many teams—including my team—we are all very mindful and sometimes we compete to do the same news.

Of course, not all news organizations use web analytics the same way, so the impact of web analytics on newsroom cultures will vary across different newsrooms. For example, a desk editor for an online-only news outlet in Hong Kong is critical of web analytics and how it might affect his reporters. "I don't want them to be page view journalists," he said. "Because when you become a page view journalist, you just ignore so much social awareness, social responsibility and also the media ethics. And I think it's very dangerous." A senior reporter for a television website in Singapore admits that it is easy to become too focused on social media metrics. "I think I speak for most, if not all, digital journalists, that we obsess a bit about Facebook to see how our stories are doing." This is why having editors to remind reporters of the organization's priorities is crucial. "It's good that we have editors around to tell us that it's not always about the numbers."

The use of audience metrics in the newsroom might also be giving rise to a "functional differentiation of journalism cultures" (Hanusch, 2017, p. 1571). This means that even within the same newsroom, different ways of doing journalism might co-exist. For example, web analytics has allowed journalists to engage in day-parting as well as platform-parting—that is, they know how audiences behave differently when it comes to news consumption depending on the time of the day as well depending on the platform they are using. As journalists respond to these metrics and package content differently to target different dayparts and platforms, "multiple production cultures may be emerging" (Hanusch, 2017, p. 1583). On top of this, some newsrooms have also added non-journalists into their editorial teams to focus on making sense of big data collected from audiences. New audience-oriented roles have also emerged in some newsrooms, such as the audience engagement editor tasked to focus on making sense of audience metrics (Ferrer-Conill & Tandoc, 2018). These new agents within the journalistic field carry with them a different set of experience, having been socialized into a different set of norms, rules, and routines. Thus, editors now work alongside those who might have been traditionally branded as outsiders but now occupy important roles in the newsroom and bring with them their own cultures.

## Journalists and their publics

Web analytics is also changing the relationship between journalists and their publics, such as audiences and advertisers. Studies have documented how journalists traditionally relied on their own subjective judgments as well as those of their family, peers, and superiors for their editorial decisions (Gans, 1979; Schlesinger, 1978). Traditional sources of audience feedback were considered to be not representative of the actual audience. Phone calls to the newsroom and letters to the editor came from a self-selected subset of the audience, while readership surveys and broadcast ratings relied on small samples of the actual audience. Newspaper circulation rates do not account for pass-on readership. Journalists were also found to dislike numbers and statistics—the form audience research usually takes (Curtin & Maier, 2001; Gans, 1979). Journalists also believed that their news judgment diverged from the news preferences of their audiences (Wulfemeyer, 1984). Many journalists also had a negative perception of audiences, overestimating their preference for superficial topics and underestimating their preference for important content (Atkin, Burgoon, & Burgoon, 1983). Finally, journalists also sought to protect their editorial autonomy from the influence of the audience (Beam, 1995; Gans, 1979). It is no surprise, therefore, that initial theorizing considered audience influence on news work as relatively weaker than other sources of influence (Flegel & Chaffee, 1971; Gans, 1979; Shoemaker & Reese, 1996; White, 1950).

But web analytics has made audience feedback more accessible, more quantifiable, more interpretable, and more visible for journalists. Web analytics data come from the actual, not just a small subset, of the online audience. Web analytics services are also designed in a way that aggregates audience data into easily understood formats. It is also plausible that by routinely seeing audience metrics, some journalists have adjusted their imaginations of who the actual audiences are and what types of content they want. For example, a comparison of how online editors in the United States rated their level of interest in different news topics and how interested they thought their audiences were in the same range of topics found that while they rated themselves as being more interested than their audiences in both public and semi-public affairs stories, they perceived their audiences to be more interested than they personally were in non-public affairs stories (Tandoc & Rosenthal, 2017). Public affairs stories referred to news stories about politics, government, and business; semi-public affairs stories referred to news stories about the environment, health, science, food, and art; while non-public affairs stories referred to news stories about crime, celebrities, sports, and weather. But the study also found that while journalists' use of social media was related to their perceived incongruence with the audience across the three topic areas, web analytics use was actually related to perceived congruence when it comes to public affairs stories (Tandoc & Rosenthal, 2017). That is, the more frequently an editor uses web analytics, the more likely for that editor to perceive that his level of interest in public affairs news is similar to that of his audiences (Tandoc & Rosenthal, 2017). So while journalists in the past perceived their audiences to be less interested in public affairs news than they themselves were, exposure to what audiences click on seems to show some journalists that this traditional perception does not really hold true.

But while web analytics allows journalists to determine which stories audiences are clicking and spending time reading, it does not explain why such behavior occurs. This still leaves a lot of room for editorial guesswork for journalists. Studies have found that even in the age of analytics, many journalists still value their editorial autonomy. For example, MacGregor (2007) argued that many journalists using web analytics still prioritized traditional news values over audience metrics in guiding story selection.

A web editor in the United States also said web analytics is "something to bounce an idea off." While I was observing at his newsroom, he showed me how Visual Revenue, the web analytics service his newsroom subscribed to, was suggesting that a celebrity news article be moved to the homepage's main story spot. The article was already going viral and moving it to the main story spot would guarantee good traffic: Visual Revenue even showed an estimated number of additional site visits the move would generate. Seeing this recommendation, the web editor clicked "decline." He turned to me and said: "You see why we don't let the machines do it?"

Learning from such responses to Visual Revenue's recommendation function, Chartbeat, another web analytics provider, had designed its dashboard "to perform deference to users' interpretive abilities and decision-making skills" (Petre, 2018, p. 517). It omitted any recommendation function that would tell users which stories to place on which spot. Doing so helps make editors using the service feel that they, and not the machine, are still in-charge. This is consistent with how much journalists value their editorial autonomy. Web analytics providers would often tell subscribers their dashboards just corroborate what journalists already know (Belair-Gagnon & Holton, 2018; Petre, 2018). It is also plausible, however, that journalists let themselves believe that they are in control by recalibrating their own editorial decisions based on the audience metrics they routinely see. By telling themselves that their news decisions are based mostly on their own news judgments, journalists protect their sense of autonomy. But what actually shapes those news judgments, especially at a time when audience feedback has become pervasive, and audience attention has become extremely important? Some journalists might be adjusting their news judgments and tailoring it more to accommodate the audience. In doing so, they feel that they remain in control.

But while many studies have focused on web analytics as a conduit for audience preferences, not a lot of studies have examined newsrooms' use of web analytics in relation to advertising, even if web analytics supplies important audience information that forms part of a newsroom's online marketing kit.

Potential advertisers look at audience metrics before deciding whether or not to buy digital advertising. Indeed, the chief editor of an online-only news outlet in Hong Kong said that advertisers are very interested in analytics. "You have a lot of advertisers out there asking you to have this analytics," she said. "And your sales team needs to have that to build a story, to talk to advertisers, to appeal for, you know, sponsors."

Web analytics serves as a platform that links journalists, audiences, and advertisers. Audiences communicate their preference to journalists through web analytics. Advertisers also prefer particular audience metrics for specific campaigns. Google ads, which account for a substantial volume of digital advertising, also automatically deploys ads and therefore revenues based on audience metrics that allow targeted advertising. With these considerations, web analytics puts advertising considerations right into the heart of the newsroom, breaking down the so-called editorial wall between the editorial and the advertising departments in many newsrooms. And by embedding audience metrics into journalistic routines, web analytics has also contributed to the increasing influence of the audience on the news construction process.

## Norms and community

But aside from exerting impacts on journalists, news content, news organizations, and the relationship between journalists and their publics (Pavlik, 2000), web analytics seems to be also affecting journalistic norms and priorities. For example, studies have explored how audience metrics influence how journalists evaluate the impact of their work (Powers, 2018) as well as how they measure news quality (Tandoc & Thomas, 2017). Norms, which refer to "moral prescriptions for social behavior" (Schudson, 2001, p. 151), can shape individual and collective behaviors (Lapinski & Rimal, 2005). The journalistic field has its own set of norms, which helps distinguish it from other fields and external forces. These norms, such as transparency and objectivity, also ideally help the pursuit of journalistic quality. But web analytics has helped facilitate the entry of a new set of logics into the journalistic field, bringing in a potentially new set of norms when it comes to evaluating quality. For example, studies have noticed the use of the phrase "doing well" in online newsrooms to describe news articles (Nelson & Tandoc, 2018; Tandoc & Thomas, 2017).

What does it mean when a news article is doing well? A survey of 206 online editors in the United States found that journalists have varying definitions (Tandoc & Thomas, 2017). Stories are described to be doing well if "a) they are getting a lot of readership; b) they are getting a lot of clicks; c) they are being shared on social media; d) people are talking about them; or e) they contribute to journalism's social functions" (Tandoc & Thomas, 2017, p. 40). Traffic-oriented definitions, however, were the most common (Tandoc & Thomas, 2017). For example, an online editor wrote in response to the question of what a story doing well means in his own newsroom:

> If it has over 3,000 hits over the course of a day, I'd say it did 'well.' If it has over 5,000 hits, I'd say it did 'very well.' If it has over 10,000 hits, I'd say it did 'great.'

Those working for larger newsrooms responded in similar ways, only with much higher thresholds in terms of number of clicks or page views (Tandoc & Thomas, 2017).

In a large newsroom in the United States, the phrase "doing well" simply meant a story is performing well based on audience metrics, as opposed to a story "doing good," which refers to normative measures of success, such as news coverage helping change policy or exposing corruption. With web analytics now institutionalized in most online newsrooms, many journalists also seem to have come to the resolution that "doing well" and "doing good" are mutually exclusive goals that they have to pursue (Nelson & Tandoc, 2018). This potentially shows an increasing awareness among some journalists that dominant uses of web analytics serve a primarily economic, rather than journalistic, purpose. By distinguishing "doing well" from "doing good," these journalists seem to recognize that the larger context that shaped, and has subsequently been shaped by, how web analytics is used in journalism "rewards and punishes news organizations based on criteria that have little to do with the public service mission of journalism" (Nelson & Tandoc, 2018, p. 14).

And that is probably what is at stake here.

When Ryan and I were working on our essay that reflected on the ethical dilemmas that come with the use of web analytics (Tandoc & Thomas, 2014), I found myself arguing with some of the arguments we put forward. Some of these internal debates can be gleaned in the concluding sections of our published work, where we go back and forth from normative theories to practical examples (Tandoc & Thomas, 2014).

We outlined three main concerns in the essay. First, we cautioned against the trap of "viewing the audience as disaggregated segments based on consumer preference" (Tandoc & Thomas, 2014, p. 244). Web analytics allows audience segmentation based on size, interests, geographic location, among others. Thus, newsrooms might prioritize local audiences that local advertisers prefer and deliver types of content that this segment of the audience wants. Other newsrooms might prioritize the majority and subsequently focus on outputs that deliver consistent audience numbers. Second, we also cautioned against "romanticizing audience choice" and considering audience metrics as goals rather than as means to serve journalism's larger social functions (Tandoc & Thomas, 2014, p. 247). Audiences do not always know what they want, more so what they need (Baker, 2002; Beam, 1995; Napoli, 2011). Thus, "acknowledging the public's greater capacity for choice should be the start of the conversation rather than the end of it" (Tandoc & Thomas, 2014, p. 248). Finally, we also called for reflections on journalistic autonomy, arguing that discourses that celebrate audience autonomy and the increase in the influence of the audience on news construction processes come at the expense of journalistic autonomy, as if arguing that the solution to the current woes of journalism is "to remove journalists from the narrative altogether and place agency in the hands of the public-as-consumer" (Tandoc & Thomas, 2014, p. 251).

My work on how journalists use web analytics has exposed me to the harsh realities that many traditional news organizations and their journalists are facing. One morning in 2013, I witnessed a Pulitzer Prize-winning photojournalist emerge out of a meeting where he was told that he had just been laid off the news company where he had worked for 23 years. The company that owned another news outlet that I visited spun off into two companies a few months after I did my research. In my interviews, observations, and surveys, I find that the adoption of web analytics is an economic rather than a journalistic strategy. The patterns of use I have seen in many newsrooms are also similarly focused on growing audiences. Ryan and I cautioned against these patterns of use (Tandoc & Thomas, 2014). But is it wrong for journalists and their news organizations to go after traffic to keep revenues stable and be able to continue doing journalism?

During one of my observations in the United States, a managing editor demonstrated to me how to use Chartbeat, the web analytics tool his newsroom used. He pointed at a news story, one he considered to be important. The story was about a six-month-old baby who was accidentally shot and killed in a drive-by shooting that purportedly targeted her father. The tragic incident showed the extent of violence in some parts of Chicago. But after a few hours, the story's page views had started to dwindle. So the managing editor shared a link to the story using his personal and the newsroom's Facebook accounts. In a few minutes, the story's number of page views started going up.

This pattern of use—keeping an eye on the metrics of an important story, one that audiences need to know, and using effective strategies to draw attention to it—is not very common, however. Other editors I sat with have accumulated different strategies that have helped their stories to attract more traffic, for example, by adding visual elements to a post, either a photo or an infographic. But more often, web analytics is used to check which stories audiences want based on metrics, so that these stories can be promoted on social media, placed more prominently on the homepage, and be the subjects of follow-up articles, to drive more traffic to site.

But what that one simple experiment showed me is that it is also possible to use web analytics to help drive traffic to stories that audiences should know and should talk about. For that's what journalism is for, to bridge differences and connect the individual to society (Tandoc & Thomas, 2014). "A major function of journalism within a democracy is the building of community" (Tandoc & Thomas, 2014, p. 244). This does not mean that news organizations should exclusively provide outputs that audiences need to know. What this means is that journalists should not be too preoccupied with providing what audiences want, pursuing what interests the public at the expense of public interest by treating audience metrics as goals instead of what they really are: Information that can guide them in pursuing the survival of *both* journalism and democracy.

## References

Arenberg, T., & Lowrey, W. (2018). The impact of web metrics on community news decisions: A resource dependence perspective. *Journalism & Mass Communication Quarterly*, 1077699018801318. doi:10.1177/1077699018801318

Armentrout, M. (2018). Chicago Tribune slashes newsroom jobs. *Chicago Sun-Times*. Retrieved from https://bit.ly/2FA0zhm

Atkin, C. K., Burgoon, J. K., & Burgoon, M. (1983). How journalists perceive the reading audience. *Newspaper Research Journal, 4*(2), 51–63.

Baker, C. E. (2002). *Media, markets, and democracy*. New York: Cambridge University Press.

Beam, R. A. (1995). How newspapers use readership research. *Newspaper Research Journal, 16*(2), 28–38. doi:10.1177/073953299501600204

Belair-Gagnon, V., & Holton, A. E. (2018). Boundary work, interloper media, and analytics in newsrooms. *Digital Journalism, 6*(4), 492–508. doi:10.1080/21670811.2018.1445001

Channick, R. (2013). Chicago Sun-Times lays off its photo staff. *Chicago Tribune*. Retrieved from https://trib.in/2HgcaDO

Curtin, P. A., & Maier, S. R. (2001). Numbers in the newsroom: A qualitative examination of a quantitative challenge. *Journalism and Mass Communication Quarterly, 78*(4), 720–738.

Edmonds, R. (2013). ASNE census finds 2,600 newsroom jobs were lost in 2012. *Poynter*. Retrieved from https://bit.ly/1in7Lst

Ehrlich, M. C. (2014). Taking animal news seriously: Cat tales in The New York Times. *Journalism, 17*(3), 366–381. doi:10.1177/1464884914561577

Ferrer-Conill, R., & Tandoc, E. (2018). The audience-oriented editor: Making sense of the audience in the newsroom. *Digital Journalism, 6*(4), 436–453. doi: 10.1080/21670811.2018.1440972

Flegel, R. C., & Chaffee, S. H. (1971). Influences of editors, readers, and personal opinions on reporters. *Journalism & Mass Communication Quarterly, 48*(4), 645–651. doi:10.1177/107769907104800404

Gans, H. (1979). *Deciding what's news* (1st ed.). New York: Pantheon Books.

Hanitzsch, T., & Vos, T. P. (2016). Journalism beyond democracy: A new look into journalistic roles in political and everyday life. *Journalism*. doi:10.1177/1464884916673386

Hanusch, F. (2017). Web analytics and the functional differentiation of journalism cultures: Individual, organizational and platform-specific influences on newswork. *Information, Communication & Society, 20*(10), 1571–1586. doi: 10.1080/1369118X.2016.1241294

Hanusch, F., & Tandoc, E. (2017). Comments, analytics, and social media: The impact of audience feedback on journalists' market orientation. *Journalism*. doi:10.1177/1464884917720305

Lapinski, M. K., & Rimal, R. N. (2005). An explication of social norms. *Communication Theory, 15*(2), 127–147. doi:10.1111/j.1468-2885.2005.tb00329.x

Lasorsa, D. L., Lewis, S. C., & Holton, A. E. (2011). Normalizing twitter: Journalism practice in an emerging communication space. *Journalism Studies, 13*(1), 19–36. doi:10.1080/1461670x.2011.571825

MacGregor, P. (2007). Tracking the online audience: Metric data start a subtle revolution. *Journalism Studies, 8*(2), 280–298. doi:10.1080/14616700601148879

Mellado, C. (2015). Professional roles in news content: Six dimensions of journalistic role performance. *Journalism Studies, 16*(4), 596–614. doi:10.1080/1461670X.2014.922276

Mellado, C., & Van Dalen, A. (2013). Between rhetoric and practice. *Journalism Studies, 15*(6), 859–878. doi:10.1080/1461670x.2013.838046

Napoli, P. (2011). *Audience evolution: New technologies and the transformation of media audiences*. New York: Columbia University Press.

Neheli, N. B. (2018). News by numbers. *Digital Journalism, 6*(8), 1041–1051. doi:10.1080/21670811.2018.1504626

Nelson, J. L., & Tandoc, E. (2018). Doing "well" or doing "good": What audience analytics reveal about journalism's competing goals. *Journalism Studies*, 1–17. doi:10.1080/1461670X.2018.1547122

Pavlik, J. (2000). The impact of technology on journalism. *Journalism Studies, 1*(2), 229–237. doi:10.1080/14616700050028226

Petre, C. (2018). Engineering consent. *Digital Journalism, 6*(4), 509–527. doi:10.1080/21670811.2018.1444998

Powers, E. (2018). Selecting metrics, reflecting norms: How journalists in local newsrooms define, measure, and discuss impact. *Digital Journalism, 6*(4), 454–471. doi:10.1080/21670811.2018.1445002

Schlesinger, P. (1978). *Putting 'reality' together.* Beverly Hills, CA: Sage.

Schudson, M. (2001). The objectivity norm in American journalism. *Journalism, 2*(2), 149–170. doi:10.1177/146488490100200201

Seow, J. (2017). SPH starts retrenching staff. *The Straits Times.* Retrieved from https://bit.ly/2TVZLq7

Shoemaker, P. J., & Reese, S. D. (1996). *Mediating the message: Theories of influences on mass media content* (2nd ed.). White Plains, NY: Longman.

Singer, J. (2005). The political j-blogger. *Journalism, 6*(2), 173–198. doi:10.1177/1464884905051009

Spence, A. (2015). Guardian faces cutbacks after 'difficult' year. *Politico.* Retrieved from https://politi.co/2FyRVQe

Spyridou, L.-P., Matsiola, M., Veglis, A., Kalliris, G., & Dimoulas, C. (2013). Journalism in a state of flux: Journalists as agents of technology innovation and emerging news practices. *International Communication Gazette, 75*(1), 76–98. doi:10.1177/1748048512461763

Steensen, S. (2011). Online journalism and the promises of new technology. *Journalism Studies, 12*(3), 311–327. doi:10.1080/1461670X.2010.501151

Tandoc, E. (2015). Why web analytics click: Factors affecting the ways journalists use audience metrics. *Journalism Studies, 16*(6), 782–799. doi:10.1080/1461670X.2014.946309

Tandoc, E., Cabañes, J. A., & Cayabyab, Y. M. (2018). Bridging the gap: Journalists' role orientation and role performance on Twitter. *Journalism Studies*, 1–15. doi:10.1080/1461670X.2018.1463168

Tandoc, E., Hellmueller, L., & Vos, T. P. (2013). Mind the gap: Between role conception and role enactment. *Journalism Practice, 7*(5), 539–554. doi:10.1080/17512786.2012.726503

Tandoc, E., & Jenkins, J. (2017). The Buzzfeedication of journalism? How traditional news organizations are talking about a new entrant to the journalistic field will surprise you! *Journalism, 18*(4), 482–500. doi:10.1177/1464884915620269

Tandoc, E., & Rosenthal, S. (2017). *What journalists think audiences want: Social media, web analytics, and journalists' perception of audience preferences.* Paper presented at the International Communication Association Conference, San Diego, California.

Tandoc, E., & Thomas, R. (2014). The ethics of web analytics: Implications of using audience metrics in news construction. *Digital Journalism, 3*(2), 243–258. doi:10.1080/21670811.2014.909122

Tandoc, E., & Thomas, R. (2017). Is "doing well" doing any good? How web analytics and social media are bringing about a new journalistic norm. *Parágrafo, 5*(2), 30–45. doi:doaj.org/toc/2317-4919

Thomas, R. (2016). In defense of journalistic paternalism. *Journal of Media Ethics, 31*(2), 86–99. doi:10.1080/23736992.2016.1152895

White, D. M. (1950). The 'gatekeeper.' A case study in the selection of news. *Journalism Quarterly, 27*, 383–390.

Westlund, O., & Ekström, M. (2018). News and participation through and beyond proprietary platforms in an age of social media. *Media and Communication, 6*(4), 1–10. doi:http://dx.doi.org/10.17645/mac.v6i4.1775

Wulfemeyer, K. T. (1984). Perceptions of viewer interests by local TV journalists. *Journalism Quarterly, 61*(2), 432–435. doi:10.1177/107769908406100231

# 6 Journalism disrupted

Web analytics was originally developed not specifically for journalism, but it is now considered a basic tool in most online newsrooms to track and understand online audience behavior (Belair-Gagnon & Holton, 2018; Petre, 2018). Tools, however, do not only facilitate certain processes: They restructure existing processes and introduce new ones. For example, news organizations have long tracked their audiences and web analytics is another tool that facilitates audience measurement. But to accommodate the flow of audience data into the newsroom in speeds and volumes unheard of before, many news organizations have also introduced new editorial positions in their organizational hierarchies, such as the audience engagement editor (Belair-Gagnon & Holton, 2018; Nelson & Tandoc, 2018). Some have also brought data scientists into their newsrooms to work alongside journalists.

Tools can also reinforce or challenge existing norms. For example, by making audience data accessible and comprehensible to news workers, web analytics reinforces audience orientation, which refers to considering audience interests in routine editorial decisions, such as in choosing topics to report about (Shoemaker & Vos, 2009). The news audience has always been closely linked to news production considerations, but while in the past news workers relied on their imaginations and constructions of the actual audience, web analytics now facilitates audience understanding by providing news workers routine and easy access to audience metrics, potentially reinforcing their orientation toward the audience. But web analytics also challenges traditional norms, such as traditional ways of evaluating news quality as well as journalistic performance. For example, the phrase "doing well" has entered the field's lexicon to refer to stories that draw high audience metrics (Nelson & Tandoc, 2018; Tandoc & Thomas, 2017), while some newsrooms reward employees based on their articles' page views (Belair-Gagnon, 2018; Tandoc & Jenner, 2016).

But understanding how tools reinforce or restructure routines and rules needs to consider how tools themselves are products of particular purposes and social contexts that shape how they are used and for what reasons. Some tools also end up being used even for purposes for which they were not originally designed. The Frisbie Pie Company in Connecticut used disk-shaped tins to hold the pies that it was selling, but in the 1950s, other people started tossing around discarded pie tins for fun and soon Frisbee became popular (Latson, 2015). Web analytics is closely associated with online marketing, where it is used to understand what factors help to convert site visits into purchases. Such conversion, however, is not as straightforward in the context of online journalism. While some news sites implement paywalls to sell particular articles or subscription packages, many news sites still rely on advertising, engaged primarily in selling audience attention to advertisers. So while tools are shaped by the purposes and social contexts within which they were created, they are also shaped by the purposes and social contexts within which they are subsequently used. Web analytics was introduced in journalism at a time when traditional news outlets were confronted by shrinking audience sizes and dwindling advertising revenues, and when online newsrooms faced an increasingly competitive digital ecosystem for audience attention. Thus, web analytics has also been understood as a mechanism to help news organizations increase traffic to ultimately improve revenues—an economic, more than a journalistic, pursuit.

Tools, therefore, are characterized by both intended and unintended uses. But who decides how it is supposed to be used and for which intended purpose? While web analytics was initially used in non-journalistic contexts, it has since been introduced to the journalistic field. Some web analytics providers, who specifically target news organizations as clients, often claim that their tools are designed in close collaboration with journalists, so that their services are tailored to the specific needs of each newsroom (Belair-Gagnon & Holton, 2018; Petre, 2018). While web analytics vendors have to please top-level editors and business managers who will have to make purchase decisions, they also have to please online editors who will be using web analytics regularly (Petre, 2018). Often, online editors align the ways they use new tools with the intended goals of their newsroom managers. But sometimes they also use new tools in ways not originally intended or envisioned. Either way, such usage patterns and the motivations underlying them are what collectively determine a new tool's impact. For example, in one of my studies, I found that the more competitive journalists perceive the market to be, the more frequently they use web analytics in their work, and the more they use web metrics to make content-related decisions (Tandoc, 2015). Indeed, a series of interviews with news managers in Sweden found that the impact of web analytics in their newsrooms is "heavily moderated by journalists and their news judgment" (Karlsson & Clerwall, 2013, p. 73).

## Conceptualizing analytics

Web analytics is more than just a simple audience tracking tool. Studies have conceptualized web analytics in journalism as: A mechanism that allows audience feedback to flow into the newsroom (Tandoc, 2014); a tool that facilitates audience quantification (Anderson, 2011); a form of "participative gatekeeping" that facilitates audience influence on news construction processes (Neheli, 2018, p. 1041); a way to implement organizational control (Cohen, 2018; Petre, 2018); and part of the move toward "the rationalization of audience understanding" (Zamith, 2018, p. 418).

Seen through the frameworks of field theory and gatekeeping, web analytics can also be conceptualized as a meeting point where the interests, motivations, and expectations of journalists, technologists, advertisers, and audiences intersect. It is a space where these agents coming from different fields encounter one another—bringing their own rules, practices, and interests—and, in the process, negotiate the contours of online journalism. Such negotiations are marked by collaborations as well as competitions, by dialogues as well as confrontations, where some interests dominate over others, changing power relations overtime. That process of negotiation is what we seek to document and understand; the outcome of that process is what we try to critically predict and prepare for.

Now embedded in most online newsrooms, web analytics has reached the point of taken-for-grantedness (Ling, 2012). Now part of many online news workers' daily routines, web analytics is no longer perceived as an object external to the journalistic field. It now forms part of online journalistic routines, shaping editorial and managerial decisions. Web analytics is no longer a new tool in journalism. Internalized by news workers, web analytics becomes potentially more influential on newsroom processes.

Web analytics can help to facilitate organizational control, as what other studies have argued (Cohen, 2018; Petre, 2018). Organizational policy works extremely well when it is implicit and therefore not questioned (Breed, 1955). Some news organizations introduced web analytics in their newsrooms with the goal of increasing online traffic (Belair-Gagnon, 2018; Tandoc, 2014). When made explicit, such organizational goals can face resistance. But through web analytics, designed to be exciting and addictive as well as to make users feel that the tool merely corroborates their news judgment, the goal of increasing traffic becomes implicit, subsumed under the cloak of control that news workers feel they have over their use of web analytics (Petre, 2018).

Web analytics can also help news workers to rationalize market-driven decisions. News selection is often idealized as the process of choosing what news audiences should read, often privileging public affairs stories. This is seen in news typologies differentiating hard news from soft news (Tuchman, 1978), as well as in the relatively less attention journalism studies pay to non-public affairs news, such as lifestyle journalism, which tends to be more popular based on metrics (Hanusch, 2019). Emerging players in the journalism industry that rose to internet fame through their viral but non-news content, such as BuzzFeed and Gawker, were initially welcomed by traditional players to the field with doubts, if not disdain (Tandoc & Jenkins, 2016, 2017). In my newsroom observations, I saw that some online editors still hesitated about, or expressed guilt right after, highlighting click-bait celebrity news stories on the homepage. I also observed a managing editor tweak an important story after finding out through web analytics that the story was not attracting a lot of traffic. But I have also witnessed how web analytics can be a way out—uncomfortable decisions can always be attributed to the machine's recommendations.

When web analytics is assumed to be located within journalism, and no longer considered as an object external to the field, news workers are more likely to accept, rather than question, its impact on journalistic rules and routines. While studies have documented how news workers normalized web analytics by using it in ways consistent with traditional practices, other studies have also demonstrated how existing rules and routines are being negotiated with emerging ones. News workers are trained to critically question news sources to get accurate information for their articles, but they usually find it challenging to question their own ways of doing.

But while we should keep an eye on how web analytics is potentially transforming journalistic rules and routines, we should also critically examine what journalistic traditions it helps to reinforce. New information technologies are not always, nor exclusively, the transformative forces that they are often presented. They can also ultimately contribute to the preservation of the status quo—of all that is good but potentially also of all that is bad. New technologies become more complicit in reinforcing existing inequalities and excesses when their perpetuative effects remain obscure, hidden under discourses focused solely on their supposedly transformative effects.

## Moving forward

Considering web analytics as the point where the various rules, practices, and motivations of journalists, news audiences, technologists, and advertisers intersect helps to identify key areas for understanding the implications for journalism. First, numerous studies have documented and analyzed how journalists use web analytics in their day-to-day work (Anderson, 2011; Bunce, 2015; Ferrucci, 2018; Hanusch, 2017; MacGregor, 2007; Neheli, 2018; Tandoc, 2014; Usher, 2013; Vu, 2013), scholarly attention that is consistent with the argument that such usage patterns affect the extent to which web analytics affects journalism. Second, some studies have also explored how web analytics and audience metrics not only represent but also subsequently affect other audiences' news preferences who consider, for example, automated lists of most popular articles as heuristics in choosing what to read (Lee, Lewis, & Powers, 2014; Thorson, 2008; Yang, 2016); others also explored what clicking actually meant for audiences themselves (Kormelink & Meijer, 2017). Third, a few studies have examined the perspective of technologists providing web analytics services to news organizations (Belair-Gagnon & Holton, 2018; Petre, 2018). However, the role of advertisers in negotiating the impact of web analytics on journalism, through the audience metrics they prioritize in deciding where to advertise, has received relatively less attention. A more in-depth look at the role that digital advertisers play will help to provide a more complete understanding of how web analytics is either preserving or disrupting journalism.

Many studies have also focused on the use of web analytics in online newsrooms, but web analytics is also used by other types of media outlets, such as magazines and wire agencies, whose target audiences are different, and therefore whose needs and usage patterns might also be different. Many studies have also focused on relatively large online newsrooms affiliated with traditional news platforms. Much smaller newsrooms might be using web analytics in different ways—for instance, focusing more on local audiences rather than mass audiences—while some might be aware of web analytics but do not use it at all, given their limited resources or different priorities, so that audiences are still tracked but using other mechanisms, potentially moderating their impact on news processes.

But we also need to clarify what we mean by impact. Now that web analytics is almost invisible in the newsroom, considered as normal and accepted as part of the routine, its impact might also become even more challenging to examine. Part of that difficulty is the challenge of defining, to start with, what we mean by impact in the context of journalism (Powers, 2018). Furthermore, most studies on web analytics have focused on examining its unintended consequences, such as how it affects newsroom cultures. In many newsrooms, however, web analytics is introduced for a specific goal, which is to help increase traffic and revenues. Studies should also revisit this assumed impact on news outlets' bottom line and examine if all the unintended consequences documented thus far were really worth it. Related to this challenge is the ongoing debate on journalism's golden metric. The online news industry has shifted from prioritizing hits and page views to focusing on unique visitors and time spent. But these metrics all have inherent limitations, so newsrooms rely on a combination of metrics, depending on their goals and priorities. These metrics also have to be weighed against how journalism as both an industry and a discipline should define and therefore measure journalistic performance.

The question then becomes not only about which metrics to measure and prioritize, but also about which journalistic norms should be considered in designing web analytics tools and deciding metrics to measure (Petre, 2018; Zamith, 2018). More normative discussions are needed to reflect on web analytics' place in journalism. For example, journalists need to listen to the audience to fulfill their social functions to sustain democracy—but up to what point? Empirical works scrutinizing how web analytics is used in the newsroom have been helpful and important, but they should be accompanied by critical and normative reflections, so that empirical findings do not get mistaken as prescriptive for the field. Instead, they should encourage a more *reflexive use* of web analytics.

In ordinary conversations, disruption simply refers to an interruption to an ongoing process. For example, a phone conversation might be disrupted by unstable reception. The conversation might temporarily halt, with the speakers suddenly caught unaware by the interruption. They would spend a few moments figuring out what happened. Such a temporary halt, often marked by confusion, would lead the speakers to try to make some adjustments to be able to continue the conversation. Or, if the adjustments don't work, they might also decide to just end the conversation and—perhaps—start a new one.

The journalistic field, it seems, is in the process of trying to figure things out. While others criticize news organizations for being too slow to respond to economic and technological shocks to the industry, what traditional journalism is experiencing is neither new nor unique. Technological innovations are also causing disruptions across other industries. In journalism, web analytics and other audience information systems have disrupted the relationships between news workers and their audiences, between editorial and advertising, and between content and technology. Such disruptions have encouraged, or perhaps forced, the journalistic field to make some adjustments. We should continue to critically examine how these adjustments—implemented by news organizations, influenced by the demands and interests of audiences, advertisers, and technologists, and enacted by journalists in their day-to-day work—impact the journalistic field.

When my proposal to conduct a content analysis to determine what content factors were associated with our newspaper's circulation figures was rejected some ten years ago, I dropped the idea right away and just resumed my work. I was curious, yes. But I was working as a newspaper reporter and audience sizes and circulation rates, I thought, were the least of my worries. Now, journalists are involved in marketing their own articles to online audiences (Tandoc & Vos, 2016). Now, journalists will find it hard not to see information about and from news audiences. They come in various forms, supplementing traditional audience information systems, from likes, shares, and comments on social media to metrics tracked by web analytics. Web analytics has disrupted journalism. It has confronted journalism's internal logic with the interests and rules of external fields, such as the technological field and the expectations of an increasingly influential audience. It has challenged journalists' traditional understanding of the audience, and consequently the power dynamics between them. Traditional ways of tracking, measuring, and conceiving of the news audience have been disrupted. But what journalism will look like after going through this, as well as through the other forms of disruptions in the field, is both an empirical and a normative question.

We need to continue analyzing analytics.

## References

Anderson, C. W. (2011). Between creative and quantified audiences: Web metrics and changing patterns of newswork in local US newsrooms. *Journalism, 12*(5), 550–566. doi:10.1177/1464884911402451

Belair-Gagnon, V. (2018). News on the fly: Journalist-audience online engagement success as a cultural matching process. *Media, Culture & Society*. doi:10.1177/0163443718813473

Belair-Gagnon, V., & Holton, A. E. (2018). Boundary work, interloper media, and analytics in newsrooms. *Digital Journalism, 6*(4), 492–508. doi:10.1080/21670811.2018.1445001

Breed, W. (1955). Social control in the newsroom: A functional analysis. *Social Forces, 33*(4), 326–335.

Bunce, M. (2015). Africa in the click stream: Audience metrics and foreign correspondents in Africa. *African Journalism Studies, 36*(4), 12–29. doi:10.1080/23743670.2015.1119487
Cohen, N. (2018). At work in the digital newsroom. *Digital Journalism*, 1–21. doi:10.1080/21670811.2017.1419821
Ferrucci, P. (2018). It is in the numbers: How market orientation impacts journalists' use of news metrics. *Journalism*, 1464884918807056. doi:10.1177/1464884918807056
Hanusch, F. (2017). Web analytics and the functional differentiation of journalism cultures: Individual, organizational and platform-specific influences on newswork. *Information, Communication & Society, 20*(10), 1571–1586. doi:10.1080/1369118X.2016.1241294
Hanusch, F. (2019). Journalistic roles and everyday life. *Journalism Studies, 20*(2), 193–211. doi:10.1080/1461670X.2017.1370977
Karlsson, M., & Clerwall, C. (2013). Negotiating professional news judgment and "clicks": Comparing tabloid, broadsheet and public service traditions in Sweden. *Nordicom Review, 34*(2), 65. doi:10.2478/nor-2013–0054
Kormelink, T. G., & Meijer, I. C. (2017). What clicks actually mean: Exploring digital news user practices. *Journalism, 19*(5), 668–683. doi:10.1177/1464884916688290
Latson, J. (2015). How Frisbees got off the ground. *Time*. Retrieved from https://bit.ly/2DKIwD3
Lee, A. M., Lewis, S. C., & Powers, M. (2014). Audience clicks and news placement: A study of time-lagged influence in online journalism. *Communication Research, 41*(4), 505–530. doi:10.1177/0093650212467031
Ling, R. (2012). *Taken for grantedness: The embedding of mobile communication into society*. Cambridge, MA: The MIT Press.
MacGregor, P. (2007). Tracking the online audience. *Journalism Studies, 8*(2), 280–298. doi:10.1080/14616700601148879
Neheli, N. B. (2018). News by numbers. *Digital Journalism, 6*(8), 1041–1051. doi:10.1080/21670811.2018.1504626
Nelson, J. L., & Tandoc, E. (2018). Doing "well" or doing "good": What audience analytics reveal about journalism's competing goals. *Journalism Studies*, 1–17. doi:10.1080/1461670X.2018.1547122
Petre, C. (2018). Engineering consent: How the design and marketing of newsroom analytics tools rationalize journalists' labor. *Digital Journalism, 6*(4), 509–527. doi:10.1080/21670811.2018.1444998
Powers, E. (2018). Selecting metrics, reflecting norms: How journalists in local newsrooms define, measure, and discuss impact. *Digital Journalism, 6*(4), 454–471. doi:10.1080/21670811.2018.1445002
Shoemaker, P. J., & Vos, T. P. (2009). *Gatekeeping theory*. New York: Routledge.
Tandoc, E. (2014). Journalism is twerking? How web analytics is changing the process of gatekeeping. *New Media & Society, 16*(4), 559–575. doi:10.1177/1461444814530541
Tandoc, E. (2015). Why web analytics click: Factors affecting the ways journalists use audience metrics. *Journalism Studies, 16*(6), 782–799. doi:10.1080/1461670X.2014.946309

Tandoc, E., & Jenkins, J. (2016). Out of bounds? How Gawker's outing a married man fits into the boundaries of journalism. *New Media & Society*. doi:10.1177/1461444816665381

Tandoc, E., & Jenkins, J. (2017). The Buzzfeedication of journalism? How traditional news organizations are talking about a new entrant to the journalistic field will surprise you! *Journalism, 18*(4), 482–500. doi:10.1177/1464884915620269

Tandoc, E., & Jenner, M. (2016). Analyzing web analytics: How newsrooms use web metrics in news construction and why. *Journal of Applied Journalism & Media Studies, 5*(3), 423–440. doi:10.1386/ajms.5.3.423_1

Tandoc, E., & Thomas, R. (2017). Is "doing well" doing any good? How web analytics and social media are bringing about a new journalistic norm. *Parágrafo, 5*(2), 30–45. doi:doaj.org/toc/2317-4919

Tandoc, E., & Vos, T. P. (2016). The journalist is marketing the news: Social media in the gatekeeping process. *Journalism Practice, 10*(8), 950–966. doi:10.1080/17512786.2015.1087811

Thorson, E. (2008). Changing patterns of news consumption and participation. *Information, Communication and Society, 11*(4), 473–489. doi:10.1080/13691180801999027

Tuchman, G. (1978). *Making news: A study in the construction of reality*. New York: Free Press.

Usher, N. (2013). Al Jazeera English online: Understanding web metrics and news production when a quantified audience is not a commodified audience. *Digital Journalism, 1*(3), 335–351. doi:10.1080/21670811.2013.801690

Vu, H. T. (2013). The online audience as gatekeeper: The influence of reader metrics on news editorial selection. *Journalism, 15*(8), 1094–1110. doi:10.1177/1464884913504259

Yang, J. (2016). Effects of popularity-based news recommendations ("most-viewed") on users' exposure to online news. *Media Psychology, 19*(2), 243–271. doi:10.1080/15213269.2015.1006333

Zamith, R. (2018). Quantified audiences in news production. *Digital Journalism, 6*(4), 418–435. doi:10.1080/21670811.2018.1444999

# Index

access and observation stage 40
actual audience 2, 12, 16, 57, 59, 60, 69
Adobe 1
Adobe Analytics 28–9
advertisers 14, 15, 43, 61–2, 70, 73
advertising model 5–6
advertising revenues 70; declining of 1, 32; in newspapers 1, 3
Anderson, C. W. 43
Ang, I. 14
audience analytics 27
audience behavior 15–16, 27, 56, 57; online 69
audience data 43, 46; accessible and comprehensible 69; estimation across websites 30–1; exposure to 2; flow into newsroom 69; tracking of 47
audience engagement editor 54, 59, 69
audience feedback: journalists attitudes toward use of 37; into newsroom, forms of 54; qualitative 42; rejection of 12–14; traditional sources of 59
audience information systems 39
audience interests 29, 69
audience measurement systems 12–13, 16, 19
audience metrics 2, 8, 46, 55, 56, 60, 61–2; accessibility and omnipresence of 56; to measure and prioritize 74; offline 27; tracking of 23; use in newsroom 59
audience-oriented roles 59
audiences: autonomy 16; communication of 62; defined as 14–16; fragmentation 16; in journalism 17–19; measurement in journalism 31; negative perception of 60
Australian Associated Press (AAP) 47

Baker, C. E. 12
Belair-Gagnon, V. 33
Benson, R. 26
big data 8, 38, 59; collection, storage, and analysis of 36
Boczkowski, P. J. 37
Bourdieu, Pierre 5, 24, 25, 31, 32
broadcast ratings 2, 13, 15, 19, 59
Bruns, A. 16
business of analytics 27–31
buyer group 32
BuzzFeed 57, 72

Canada, local newsroom in 56, 58
capital concept 25–6
cat posts 57
Champagne, Patrick 4
Chartbeat 28, 30–3, 36, 61, 64
circulation rates 15, 59
Clerwall, C. 47
community 62–5
"comprehensive value system" 43
Comscore 31
consumer orientation 56
content contribution 17–18
content customization 18–19
content dissemination 18
content-oriented use 45

"cookies" 38
crowdsourcing 17
cultural capital 26, 32, 37

data denialists 46
data-informed journalists 46
day-today journalism: access and observation stage 40; deselection process 41; distribution stage 41–2; interpretation stage 42; processing/editing stage 41; selection/filtering stage 40–1; *see also* journalism
deselection process 41
desk editors 57, 58
digital editor 56–7
digital-first mind-set 4
digital journalism 4, 40, 41
distribution stage 41–2
"doing good" phrase 8, 63
"doing well" phrase 7, 63, 69
Domingo, D. 42
doxa 24–5, 27
Duterte, Rodrigo 5

economic capital 26, 28, 32
economic uncertainties 4
editorial analytics 27
"editorial crack" 36, 48–9
editorial guesswork 2, 37–40
editorial meetings: "doing well" phrase 7; in newsrooms 40
"engagement editor" 38
Estrada, Joseph 4
Ettema, J. 15
exposure-based audience measurement techniques 16

Facebook 5, 30, 42
field concept 24
field theory 32; focus on autonomy 27; forms of capital 25–6; frameworks of 24–7, 71
*The Financial Times* (FT) 30
Frisbie Pie Company 69
full-time journalists 53

Gans, H. 12
gatekeeping process 24, 41–2, 71
gatekeeping theory 5–6, 11, 24
Gawker Media 32, 43, 72
Gillies, Tony 47
Google ads 62
Google Analytics 28, 36
*The Guardian* 29
Guardian News & Media 29–30

habitus 24, 25, 27
Hardin, M. 16
headline-testing service 41
Hermida, A. 18
hits 8, 38, 74
Holton, A. E. 33
Hong Kong: "comprehensive value system" 43; desk editor for online-only newsroom in 23, 57, 58; digital editor in 56–8

individual journalists 7, 37, 46, 55
information and communication technologies 19
institutionalization, of web analytics 31–2, 54
"institutionalized audience" 14
interpretation stage 42
"invented audience" 12

journalism: audiences in 17–19, 31; conceptualization of 5; conceptualized web analytics in 71–2; digital 4, 40, 41; disruption of 6–8; as a field 24–7; normative roles of 31; potential negative impact on 48; *see also* day-today journalism
journalistic doxa 25, 40
journalistic field 6, 24–8, 31–3, 48, 54, 59, 62, 70, 71, 74, 75
journalists: adopting and adapting 37–8; and audiences preferences 13; balancing act of 7; data-informed 46; full-time 53; impact on 54–6; individual 7, 37, 46, 55; pejorative view of audience 14; political influence to 5; and their publics 59–62; usage of web analytics 64; value and protecting autonomy 14; working procedure of 52

Karlsson, M. 47

Lantern 30
legacy news organizations 4, 37

MacGregor, P. 61
market orientation 47–8
mass audience 16, 73
media systems 36
multi-layered gatekeeping process 24

Napoli, P. 16
Neveu, E. 26
news audiences 17, 19, 31, 41, 69, 72, 73, 75
news content 18, 37, 56–8; indirect influence on 11–12; nature of 53; reshaping of 41
news editors 40
news organizations 2, 5, 19, 26, 42, 69; differences between 47; market orientation 47; newsroom management 43; online community study 13; in Singapore 43–4
newspapers: advertising revenues 1, 3; circulation rates in United States 3; reporters 52–3
newsroom analytics 27
newsroom ethnographies 44
newsroom management 43, 45
newsrooms: analytics tools in 23; audience metrics use in 59; comparision, on metrics 7; editorial meetings in 40; in Hong Kong 23; loyal *vs.* local readers 43; in United States 31, 37, 44, 47, 55, 57, 63; web analytics in 36
news selection 6, 11, 41, 57, 72
*The New York Times* 30, 32
non-news content 72
norms 62–5; tools to reinforce/challenge existing 69

*The Observer* 29
offline audience metrics 27
off-site web analytics 30
Omniture 1
one-time visitors 43
online audiences 75; behavior 69; characteristics and behavior of 2; web analytics data 60
online editors 32, 42, 54, 55, 57–8; focus on real-time metrics 46; in Singapore 43; in United States 60; web analytics tools purchase 70
online journalism 70; negotiation process 6, 71
online journalists: skills and educational credentials of 26; workload for 55
online newsrooms 36, 38, 46, 47; management of 43
online-only news outlet 57, 58, 61–2
online platform 3, 37
online sites 38
on-site web analytics 30
Ophan 29–30
organizational culture 7, 37, 58–9
outgoing ads 29

page views 38, 58, 64–5, 74
Parse.ly 29
Parse.ly Analytics 29
Parse.ly Dash 29
Pavlik, J. 53
pay-per-click model 3
peoplemeters 15
Petre, C. 32
*The Philippine Daily Inquirer* 1, 4, 8
processing/editing stage 41
produsers 16
public affairs stories 60

qualitative audience feedback 42

readership surveys 2, 13, 15, 16, 19
real-time metrics 17, 46
Reese, S. D. 40

search engines 5
selection/filtering stage 40–1
Shoemaker, P. J. 40
SimilarWeb 29
Singapore: interviews with journalists in 48; news organization in 43–4; online editors in 43; social media editor in 47
social media 40; accounts 18; analytics 27; platforms 2, 3, 5, 19; promoting content on 42; sites 42
Stela 30
*The Straits Times* 4

technological adoption 37
technological innovation 53, 54, 74

television ratings 13, 15
third-party web analytics services 37
Thomas, Ryan 63, 64
time spent 39, 74
traditional audience measurement techniques 15
traditional journalism 37, 40, 48, 74
traffic-oriented use 45
Twitter 18, 30, 42, 53–4

unique visitors 38–9, 41, 74
United States: newspapers circulation rates in 3; newsrooms in 31, 37, 44, 47, 55, 57, 63; online editors in 60, 62–3; web editor in 61
Urchin Software Corporation 28
user comments 18, 42
user-generated content 17, 18, 41

Visual Revenue 61

web analytics 1, 27, 36; basic tool in online newsrooms 69; changes and continuities 44–6; conceptualization of 71–2; in digital-native and traditional newsrooms 47; ecosystem 23; embedded in news routines 8; as form of technology 32; frequency of using 45; gaps in 39; homepages of 2; implications for local coverage 58; installation of 31; institutionalization of 31–2; journalists usage of 64; news managers sense of audiences 43; in newsrooms 36; off-site 30; on-site 30; provides readers' geo-location details 43; shaping usage patterns 46–8; usage of 40–5; use for management purposes 55–6
web analytics data 38, 44, 46, 48, 56, 60
web analytics firms 32, 33
web analytics programs 2, 41
web analytics tools 23, 28–30; availability and accessibility of 47; intended and unintended uses 70; in newsrooms 23
web editor, in United States 58, 61
web metrics: commonly tracked 39; selection of 38–9
website analysis 29
Webtrekk 29
Whitney, D. C. 15
wire agencies 47, 73
The Worlds of Journalism Study 31

Zamith, R. 27

9781032338354